Sell Your Home for Top Dollar

DAN BLANDING

ISBN-13: 9780692134856
ISBN-10: 0692134859
Library of Congress Control Number: 2018907847
Silver Sea Publishing, Pasadena, California

Disclaimer: The opinions and suggestions set forth in this book are just that: our opinions and our suggestions. This is based on decades of observation and experience in the real estate sales industry. The scenarios in this book have been used to help drive home points and come from an accumulation of over thirty years in selling homes. Although the essence and gist are there, narrative license and paraphrasing have been used; in addition, names and circumstances have been changed or altered to protect the privacy of the individual(s). This book is not intended to give you legal or tax advice. It is our recommendation that if you are considering selling or buying a home, seeking appropriate legal, tax and financial advice from reputable professionals would be a good course of action. Further, aside from the obvious unethical or illegal acts some real estate agents may unfortunately perform, this book is in no way a put down toward how other agents conduct business. We are all different—real estate agents, that is—and that uniqueness expresses itself in each individual's particular services. We have our own way of working with sellers that has proven successful over decades. Much of this book includes laying down some general systems that we try to use. We hope our thoughts, opinions and observations will hopefully give you some structure as well as food for thought as you begin the process of hiring a real estate agent for the job of selling your home.
Dan Blanding, DRE 00874833; Joy Cross, DRE 00915798; Remax Masters, DRE 01064901.

To all our past clients who over the decades have shown consistent support and loyalty, we appreciate you and never take your kindness, referrals and trust for granted!

CONTENTS

PREFACE

I truly love the real estate industry. I am extremely grateful to it for providing me of course with not only a wonderful job but also a fulfilling career that has allowed me the opportunity to work with people from all walks of life. We have been hired by homeowners who retained our services to help them not only with the sale of their home but also with the sale of one of the largest assets that they may ever own; this is without a doubt a huge responsibility and not one to be taken for granted. It is truly wonderful to know that we are trusted on this level, especially in an industry that has unfortunately suffered, well, let's just call it, some reputation issues.

It was this challenge of overcoming a certain stigma that was partly the reason I felt compelled to write this book. I want the community of homeowners to know that there are indeed very qualified professionals out there who will make your selling experience not only easier but also much more profitable; in the end, however, finding these agents can often be a challenge. We will address that.

Many times I have been approached by homeowners well outside my service area. Although I cannot personally help them sell their home, they still contact me. It may go something like this: "Dan, I want to sell my home. I have no idea where to start; I've read stuff online, but quite honestly, there is too much information and too many agents claim to be number one. How do I even start on this process? Help!"

My goal in this book is to *help* you, no matter what part of the country you are in, to easily locate, interview, and hire the absolutely best agent for the job of selling your home.

I've been watching agents come and go out of this business for decades, and I have articulated my own way of segregating them down into four different categories, which we will discuss in chapter 2.

My point for the time being is this: in order to choose the right agent, you must choose not only a good and decent human being but also a professional who has the skills, reputation, and experience to successfully get the job done—that is, where it pertains to selling your home. I've written this book with an easy point-by-point system to make the locating and hiring of an agent a smooth, simple, step-by-step process that should lead you to a successful end.

I would like to take this opportunity to address a few things regarding our personal services. I suspect the vast majority of my readers are out of our geographical area of service—that is, we cannot help you sell your home. I'm sorry; we would love to work with you! Unfortunately we only service certain areas within Southern California. Our team can, however, have a like-minded agent contact you, if you so desire. There is no charge to you for this service. Please reference the very last couple of pages of this book, titled "A Final Note from the Author and Contact Information," for details.

Thank you for your trust, evidenced by your purchase of this book, and I am confident you will find many, if not all, of your answers in the pages to follow.

HOW TO READ AND WHAT TO EXPECT FROM THIS BOOK

You will note this book is about getting top dollar for your home by hiring the right real estate agent to sell your home. This is not about agents who work with buyers; this is not a book about the closing process.

We touch on marketing, but this is not about real estate marketing, per se. Further, this is certainly not a get-rich-quick plan about investing in real estate. Rather, it's a book about one subject in a very large and complex industry.

Make no mistake; this is a job interview. In a sense, you are the employer, and the real estate agent is the prospective employee who will be attempting to convince you to hire him or her. Yes, a real estate agent may be an independent contractor, but I am simply using the employer/employee metaphor as an example to help you get a better idea what both your roles are.

Think about it: employers *do not* use their valuable time to interview just anyone. Instead they use due diligence to narrow down the interviewees to only a handful, a few who have the strong credentials necessary to even be considered for the job. That is how I want you to view this book. You own a business; that business is your home. As the owner of your business, you have a very important decision to make—which employee, again metaphorically speaking, is going to help make your business a success. It's as simple as that.

I have purposely written this book in a direct-to-the-point manner. I could go on endlessly about the hiring process in the real estate sales industry, but rather I have chosen a simple approach. Why? Human nature. I suspect that if you are holding this book in your hands, it's not for some casual reading on your day off; rather, you are interested in selling your home. That said, I can tell you from many, many years of experience that anyone *even considering* selling his or her home has an overabundance of things going on at one time, and sitting down and reading a long-drawn-out book about hiring a real estate agent is probably not very realistic.

The Best Way to Read This Book
This book can be read in just a few sittings, which is what I would suggest. Then you can go back to it for reference purposes, if necessary. If time really does not allow, simply browse the table of contents; a subject that may apply to your own personal needs will most likely jump right out at you.

At the very least, however, I would *strongly* urge you to read chapter 4, which has contributions from my partner, Joy. The way she articulates the questions you should ask, how to prepare, and finally how to facilitate an interview with a real estate agent is simply unmatched in my opinion.

Finally, instead of referring to "real estate agent" for logistics purposes, we will often use the simpler term "agent". Now agents might be brokers, own their own brokerage, or work under a broker. For example, I may state that an "agent" is charging a certain commission when in fact, if the agent is working under a brokerage it is the brokerage that is actually charging the commission but again, for logistics and an easier reading experience, we will mostly refer to all of the above as "agents". Always refer to the National Association of REALTORS ® and your states rules about real estate agents, REALTORS® , and brokers and their respective duties, restrictions, and capacities as well as how to request licensing status.

That said, for the purposes of an easier reading experience, we will for the most part refer to all of them as simply "agents."

I do at this juncture want to also clear up something that most people I come in contact with seem to get a bit confused about, and that is the difference between a real estate agent and a REALTOR®. I will simply defer to the National Association of REALTORS® regarding the technical definition of a REALTOR®:

> The term REALTOR® has one, and only one, meaning: REALTOR® is a federally registered collective membership mark which identifies a real estate professional who

is member of the NATIONAL ASSOCIATION OF REALTORS® and subscribes to its strict Code of Ethics.

So all REALTORS® are real estate agents, but not all real estate agents are REALTORS®. Hmm, now which one do you think I am going to recommend you use? An agent who subscribes to the strict code of ethics of the National Association of REALTORS® would be a smart bet!

What You Can Really Expect from This Book

Before we dive into chapter 1, I want to give you an overview of sorts as to what you should be expecting in the pages to follow. Also, we will be using the term "systems" repeatedly. To have anything end successfully, systems must be in place, and this includes the hiring of an agent. I have articulated in a very simple way, six crucially important factors that make up the real estate agent hiring process. They are as follows:

1. *Problems and Issues*

   They are inevitable; it is simply the nature of the business. There are lots and lots of moving parts in a real estate transaction. Yet, many would-be problems can very easily be avoided if the homeowner choses the right real estate agent. Unavoidable problems? Yes, they happen, and when they do, a professional will know how to deal with them directly and calmly.

2. *Needs*

   Your particular and personal needs are going to come into play, so you can easily match an agent with those needs. One agent may be perfect for one person but completely inappropriate for someone else. I will help you define your needs.

3. *Types of Agents*

   You will be educated about some different types of real estate agents out there. I will also give you opinions on who I feel are the best to interview for your specific needs. Even though you will learn which is the best type of agent for *you*, you are still going to have to know how to find that agent. There may be dozens, hundreds, or perhaps even thousands of real estate agents in your area. Although narrowing down only a few may seem like an impossible task, I can tell you right now that it is not. I am going to show you how to do this.

4. *Interview Preparation*

Once you have narrowed down a few agents to interview and have matched them up with your needs, you will need to prepare for that interview. You can rest assured that the agent will (or should) be prepared. This is very easy if you know how; you will be learning simple techniques to prepare as well as vital questions to ask.

5. *The Actual Interview*

During the interview process you need to know what to expect, what to look for, what to ask, and how to handle yourself in general. My partner, Joy, and I will be teaching you some very basic and easy ways in which to do that.

6. *After You Have Hired an Agent*

Once you have chosen an agent, it does not end there. You will need to make sure that everything that the agent promises you will be done. There is a simple yet successful way to ensure this. It's always very important that you are educated by your agent so that you at least have a working knowledge of what happens after the fact—that is, after you have entered into a contract with a broker.

So there are the bare bones of what you will be learning. Now let's go ahead and get started and move on to chapter 1; enjoy and learn, and as a result, I am confident you will have a successful and profitable real estate sales experience!

Buy land, they're not making it anymore.

—*Mark Twain*

1

DO NOT LET THIS HAPPEN TO YOU!

I've been witness to just too many things that have happened in a real estate transaction. Once a homeowner signs with another broker, in most cases and depending on the contract, it would be unethical for me to involve myself. Instead sometimes I have to witness a train wreck, one that I know could have been easily avoided had the seller just taken precautions during the agent hiring process. The worst situation would of course be problems that come up after the fact, meaning, after the close of escrow. This is extremely problematic, and with the wrong agent, the likelihood of that increases. The right agent will make sure that the odds of something like this happening are extremely low. During the escrow period, although it can be very frustrating, at least issues have a chance to be resolved. Afterward? Something you most definitely want to avoid, and it can be very avoidable.

Challenges Most Certainly Do Exist
Following are examples of just a few of the many problems that can sometimes surface in a real estate transaction. Of course, not all transactions are going to have multiple issues like this, but I have yet to have seen one real estate deal that did not have some kind of difficulty or complications, it's simply the nature of the business.

This section is in no way meant to frighten you or make you nervous about selling a home or even buying a home for that matter. Rather this section is meant to help you see that a lot of things can happen during a property sale, which is why it is so vitally important to hire a professional.

Problems happen in life; there is simply no getting around that. Having the right tools to deal with those problems is crucial for satisfaction and peace of mind. But why deal with life issues that could have been prevented? A real estate transaction is *no* different. A good agent can prevent issues from even happening in the first place. For the unavoidable dilemmas and difficulties...well, that same agent will proceed to address the issue and will move forward to try to solve it in an expedient, calm, and confident manner. When a problem surfaces, the expert may think along these lines, for example, "Okay, here's another challenge; this is where I am highly skilled, and this is what my client is paying me for."

There are some agents who adopt these types of mantras and continually remind themselves of their responsibilities. This is as opposed to a less professional agent who would think more along these lines: *"Ah geez, you have got to be kidding me! Really? Now I have to deal with this before I get paid!"* Yep, there are a lot of agents who sing this tune too!

This thought process would be more the reaction of nervous agents; they can truly be one of the worst to work with. Nervous agents make everyone else equally if not more nervous. How would you feel if your pilot hit some turbulence, got on the speaker, and spoke in a very nervous, shaky voice or even walked out onto the aisle looking pale as a ghost? You had better believe that you and the passengers are going to be just a bit uptight. Competent, experienced pilots, on the other hand, are going to sound very soothing; they will speak with an air of complete confidence. They have flown many, many flights and have given you no reason whatsoever to doubt that they will take you to a safe landing. That is how I want you to view the agent you decide to hire, like the pilot of a plane you are about to board.

So, let's all be witnesses for the next few moments to examples of obstacles, oversights, and miscommunications that can surface in different phases of a real estate transaction.

We'll start with the buyer in scenarios that happened *after* that buyer agreed to purchase the property. But first let me tell you that a skillful agent will always make sure anything pertinent is fully disclosed to the buyer. I think good agents would always want to see buyers of their clients' homes have a professional inspection of the property. I doubt that this type of listing agent or their clients would have ever seen the inside of a courtroom. But sometimes a buyer does not have a professional inspection or the inspector misses something or was unable to check certain things because of inaccessibility. Sometimes potential issues are innocently overlooked by the homeowner, and they end up surfacing later, deep into the escrow transaction; the list goes on. The buyer of a home can have legitimate concerns, and they must be handled efficiently, truthfully, and calmly. Although a serious matter indeed, let's still try to have a little fun with this. Here are some sample remarks from buyers after their offer was accepted.

"Is that stuff in the bathroom and kitchen mold, and the dangerous type? I think I'm getting a headache!"

"Was there an unpermitted addition on this property? Looking at it again, this house sure does look like it had some kind of add-on."

"Hey, it looks like those are high-voltage power lines above your home; what's up with that?"

"Is it my imagination? It looks like maybe your house is slanting a little; is there a soil problem?"

"Why has the water level in the pool gone down so fast? Is there a leak?"

"I drove by the house Saturday evening, and there were a bunch of teenagers smoking and drinking at the corner; does this happen a lot? Your neighbor said it does." (We'll address nosy neighbors a little later in this chapter.)

"Is this house under a flight pattern? It's like every time I look up I see a plane."

"Hey, Mr. and Mrs. Seller, I know your home is vacant, so I drove by last night, and I saw a homeless-looking person in the kitchen." (By the way, squatters can be a real issue.) I have seen many vacant properties over the years suddenly "occupied" by an uninvited guest, another situation that can easily be avoided.

"Your neighbor said there was a recent death on the property; is that true? You didn't tell us that. Was this natural or violent? Either way, I'm kind of freaked out now!"

"That fireplace is not up to code; as a matter of fact, now I'm concerned that a lot of things are not up to code."

"Did I just hear a train?"

"Is it my imagination, or did I smell something outside the house? Is there a gas leak, or are we close to a landfill or refinery? I think I'm getting another headache!"

This is just a *very* small sampling of concerns that could arise from your buyer. I can go on endlessly, but the point I am trying to make is that the unexpected can and most likely will rear its head during the sale; it really is kind of just the normal course of events in a real estate transaction, but most of these issues could have been entirely avoided in the first place and the ones that could not? Well, there is a way to handle them, and agent panicking is not of them.

Outside Influences
Now, I am not referring to legal, tax or professional financial advise entities, rather I am addressing non professional and often unsolicited input from outside person(s). I completely respect and understand people outside

the transaction wanting to step in and help, but often they do anything but. Parents can sometimes be the worst because their mind-sets can often be dated. For instance, they might remember when one could buy a house for much less than half of what they are going for now. They may kill a deal in their "ignorance" (and I use that word respectfully, but often that is just what it is) only to find out, after their kids have been renting for twenty years, that the same house has again doubled in value! Thanks a lot, Mom and Dad.

Neighbors—while some are just trying to be honest and helpful, some—can be downright nosy, dishonest, and sometimes vindictive. I may be paraphrasing, but rest assured, this kind of thing can and does happen.

"Your neighbor told me she thinks you deal in drugs."

"Your neighbor told me this neighborhood gets really loud at night."

"Your neighbor told me the police are always at your property."

"Your neighbor told me you hate your house and that is why you are selling."

"Your neighbor told me he thinks you're a spy." (Yep, neighbors can sometimes say the darndest things.)

"Your neighbor told me this and that and this and that. I don't think I believe any of it, but at the same time, do I really want this person as a neighbor?"

"My parents told me this is the wrong time to buy and I'm paying too much for this house."

"My parents told me you should pay all my closing costs; I know we signed a contract, but will you? I mean, Mr. Seller, will you pay all my closing costs?"

"My parents told me they are reconsidering giving me money to help with the down payment unless I ask you to reduce the price ten percent!" (The likely response from the seller is "Take a hike," and kids end up moving in with Mom and Dad.)

"My parents told me the market is about to crash."

"My uncle told me…"

"My great aunt who owns a bunch of real estate told me…"

"My dentist told me…"

"My psychologist told me…"

"My five-year-old told me…!"

Can some of this guidance be good, or should these things be looked into? Well, of course, yes on both counts, but what I do not want to see happen is for anyone to act immediately on that new information or advice. Rather, they should look at things carefully and methodically and make an educated decision. Remember, you are most likely hearing these questions from the agent who is representing you. An outstanding agent will make sure that your buyer or your buyer's agent is not acting too impulsively. If buyers truly trust their agents, many of these problems can be overcome.

I want at this juncture to reference another word you will hear mentioned quite often in this book, and that is "trust," albeit, yes, an overused word in any sales and service industry, including, of course, real estate, but all the same, it must be addressed in the context of the book. We will go into more detail about this word in chapter five but for now, understand that I am not speaking of "blind trust," rather a trust that must be earned. In no way should you just take agents at their word that you can trust them. But the dilemma you may run into is that you won't really know if you can trust an agent until you are well into the transaction, and then it may be too late. So what do you do? It almost seems like you are putting the cart before the horse. "Trust me," says the real estate agent; "Hire me, and I will prove to you that I am trustworthy." Well, there again, what comes first? The hiring or the trust? There is an easy way to overcome this as I will articulate in more detail throughout this book, but the bottom line is you can have legitimate, eyes wide open trust for an agent well before you hire the person.

Let's get back to some examples of challenges, problems, and concerns that can surface throughout any real estate transaction. This time we are going to listen in on both the buyers' and sellers' reactions as things were *discovered* in the closing process.

Discovery

Once the house goes into escrow, lots and lots of wheels start turning and paperwork is constantly being shuffled back and forth; things are researched and checked, and often problems are discovered. I'm going to play around with this for a little. Here are some sample responses from both the seller and the buyer as challenges arise throughout the closing process. We will start with the seller this time.

The Seller Reacts to Discovery

"But I paid that loan off twenty-five years ago! You are telling me that title found that the old deed of trust was still on the property and Clyde's Loan Service went out of business fifteen years ago? What now?"

"No, that's not true; my ex-husband's sister's boyfriend can't be on title, although I do recall something about him loaning us money a while back, but…"

"I was going to tell you I was five months behind on my payments, but I was too embarrassed; you're saying I'm being foreclosed on? I called my lender, and some guy told me they would for sure hold off on that. His name? I don't know; should I have gotten his name? All I know is that he said he worked in the collection department and that everything *should* be fine."

"I never knew there was a class action suit against the builder. Well, come to think of it, I do remember something about the neighbors not being happy about leaking roofs, but I had no problem, so I totally ignored it."

"No, that lawsuit was settled years ago; my attorney told me it would not affect my home. You're saying that title found something and the person I was in a lawsuit with is dead? But what now? My attorney is dead too!"

The list can go on. Sometimes homeowners innocently forget or are not even aware of things that can affect the salability of their property. Perhaps they purchased the property years ago, and they truthfully just forgot. When the complications come up, and they do, they must be dealt with and dealt with—you guessed it—calmly.

Now let's listen to some buyer responses.

The Buyer Reacts to Discovery
"No, no, you're wrong; that was two ex-wives ago. That was settled in the divorce; you're telling me there's a judgment against me?"

"My lender said there is a lawsuit pending between one of the homeowners and the association, and they said the lender won't do the loan!"

"But the car salesperson was pushy, and I really like convertibles; are you saying I should not have bought a Porsche while in the process of getting a home loan?"

"No, that credit card company told me when I settled with them that everything would be okay with my credit." A name? No, should I have gotten a name?

"My lender's appraiser said this house is not worth what I am paying for it."

"Well, yes, I cosigned for my brother for that condo in Florida, but it was his condo, not mine; my brother never told me it foreclosed."

"I didn't know I was supposed to *tell* you the money was *outside* the country."

"Well, yes, maybe. 'Technically,' I was out of work for six months."

"My lender said they thought the interest rates would go down, so I did not lock in the rate; yesterday the market went crazy and not in a good way; I sincerely cannot afford the payment with that new rate."

"I told you I have the money for a down payment, but it's in the antique bicycle my grandfather left me." (Yep, that one happened to me during one of my first few years in the business; I will completely admit that this should not have happened. Newer agents can often unknowingly and innocently cause a lot of problems. Fortunately, for me and my client, that bicycle was a true rarity, and it sold in a flash; my client got lucky, and I dodged a major bullet and in doing so learned a valuable lesson.)

Just like with the homeowner, these were situations that were more than likely innocent. The buyer probably did not intentionally seek out to mislead anyone, but that does not negate the fact that we now have a problem.

Problems Can Be Avoided
I do, at this juncture, want to make a very important point. Although it's true there are some things that do surface throughout the process, for the most part, the vast majority of these findings could have and really should have been discovered early on, like in the example of the antique bicycle with yours truly. Once a property is listed, the right real estate agents are going to do some investigating of their own to preempt any would-be problems. Yes, there are ways to handle that loan that was paid off twenty-five years ago but still shows up on the house, but sometimes things like this can take time to resolve. The time to address issues like this is not a few days before escrow is supposed to close.

With regard to the buyer, the right listing agent will not go on the word of the buyer or the buyer's agent; rather he or she will perform due diligence and make sure that the buyer's credit is thoroughly checked, the money verified, and that there has been ample and acceptable communication with the buyer's lender regarding his or her qualifications before escrow is even opened.

Truly, who needs the aggravation? I mean, no one is perfect; certain things can slip by even the best of agents. The point I am trying to make is that it is imperative to limit these problems as much as is humanly possible. A real estate sale even under the best of circumstances can still be challenging; agents need systems. There should be a system that goes into place the minute a homeowner signs the listing contract and another system that goes into place the second an acceptable offer is made on the property and a third system that will take you successfully through the closing process and even beyond.

It is like going on a long road trip. You don't just climb in the car and go. You need to plan, you need supplies, the trip must be properly navigated, your home needs to be secured, and you need to let loved ones know you'll be gone, where you are going, and so forth. Real estate agents should not just list homes and let things happen as they may. They should not allow *their* clients to accept offers from buyers without kicking the tires to make sure the whole thing is viable.

I am very confident that what you learn in this book will help keep at bay most obstacles because you are going to choose the right agent who will act earnestly, resulting in problems being dealt with earlier and not later. The issues that simply come out of nowhere—well, they will be addressed and most likely overcome. This does not have to be a bad experience for you, and with the right agent it will not be; rather, it will be an exciting experience, somewhat stressful, yes, but nonetheless a positive move in your life, as it should be.

"He that is of the opinion money will do everything may well be suspected of doing everything for money"

—*Ben Franklin*

2

THE PERFECT REAL ESTATE
AGENT FOR YOU

Over my thirty-year-plus span in the real estate industry, I have observed agents in very close quarters. I've seen many of them come and go. I've witnessed agents who have stood the test of time and have held strong under the most difficult market climates. I've witnessed agents who clearly took advantage of the client. Conversely, I've observed agents help their clients way past the point of obligation. For the purposes of this book, I have narrowed down four types of real estate agents I have observed over the years.

Four Types of Agents

The Good
These agents are just as the word describes. They are good! They join the real estate industry because they truly love people and selling homes is a way for them to do what they love and help people attain one of the most important investments (both emotionally and financially) in their life. They will get the job done; they're good agents, and they make a living out of doing what they enjoy. I like it, but let's read on.

The Bad

Of course, you know these agents; they're bad because they do bad things. They have little conscience when it comes to an innocent and unsuspecting home seller. For these agents, the end always justifies the means. That end could and often does leave the homeowner shortchanged in many ways. They are *obsessed* with getting paid, no matter what they must do.

Don't think for a minute that this kind of thinking is not out there; it may be in different forms, but the gist of the thought processes, delusions, and justifications is very real. "Bad" can mean a lot of different things: illegal actions, neglect, complete irresponsibility, and the list goes on. My goal here is not to scare you; rather, I want you to know this *does* exist. Fortunately, the industry does try to stop this kind of behavior.

The Ugly

These agents are certainly not good, but really, they are often not bad either. You may ask, "How can an ugly agent not be bad?" We will define "ugly" in various ways within the context of this book. Let us take laziness, for example. Laziness can certainly lead to ugly things happening. Nonchalant, yeah, that can get result in ugly; these agents are not really taking you or their job seriously. Selling a home is a very serious matter. Protection? Sure, they'll try to get everything signed properly…eventually anyway; they'll get to it maybe tomorrow or later in the week, but right now they have other things they're concerned with. You get my point.

Throughout the real estate process, if things are not taken care of in a timely manner, it can get ugly, very ugly and very fast. Try having to cancel your movers. You may need to sheepishly ask them, "Are you available, maybe next weekend?" Worse, try letting the owners of the property you are buying know that they too must cancel their movers, and oh yeah, you better call the utility companies and tell them to nix that disconnection. Wait, your interest rate is only good until the day we were supposed to close? Oh well, what's an extra ½ percent over the next thirty years? I call these agents ugly, certainly not in a literal sense, and not because they are committing some kind of crime like bad agents might but rather because the things they do or *do not do* can cause ugly things to happen.

The Outstanding Agent
Here you go—this is the agent you want. They take good to the next level. They do what they say and when they say they'll do it. They call you, not the other way around. These agents take their jobs *very* seriously and most importantly love what they do. They're the professionals; they have mastered communication skills.

If you have an outstanding agent, does that mean you can sit back and relax because everything is going to be just fine? No, you cannot. Real estate transactions have lots of moving parts; it's just that these agents understand that fact, and if something goes awry, they know how to fix it, and if for whatever reason they can't fix it, they will surely find someone more knowledgeable than themselves to get it taken care of. They are very confident in themselves, but not in an egocentric or arrogant manner. They have no ego to deal with; they have no problem asking questions when questions *must* be asked. Outstanding agents are like fine Swiss watches—very accurate, very dependable. You can count on them 100 percent of the time.

But, you may ask, "Dan, seriously, does an agent like this really exist?"

Short answer: "No, what I have described above is the perfect super-hero agent, who is nonexistent."

No one is perfect; we all have our positive and negative traits, but there are many agents who have numerous qualities of the outstanding agent as follows:

- Lots of experience
- Proper skills for your particular needs
- Professionalism
- Vast knowledge
- Trustworthiness
- A personable and friendly attitude
- A great reputation
- Lots of confidence (this one is extremely important; they are just like that pilot we mentioned earlier. They have done this many,

many times before and have little to no doubt they will get the job done right and bring you to a safe and successful landing.)

That is what I want you to look for: *qualities* that hugely outweigh deficiencies. Even with certain human character flaws, which again, each and every one of us have, I am still going to refer to these agents as outstanding because that is just what they are. You can hire a good agent if you like; it should be, we hope anyway, a *relatively* safe bet, but do try to avoid ugly agents, and run as fast as you can from bad agents. Outstanding agents, however? Latch on to one, that is, if you are able to find one, and you should, if you follow the simple methods that I have outlined in this book.

So now that you understand my opinions of the four types of agents out there, you may ask, "How do I go about finding anyone even close to being an outstanding agent?" You can easily do this. Any good detective will use the process of elimination to solve a crime. Similarly, you need to start eliminating agents before you start the narrowing-down process. We have already alluded to the good, the bad, and the ugly. There is a lot of gray area here, but let's at least try to eliminate what I feel are some of the weaker agents; you can mix in the ingredients any way you like depending on your personal situation.

Agents to Consider Eliminating

"I'm All about Old School" Agents
This old-school guy or gal is afraid of technology; he or she fought it in the nineties and is still fighting it. You may want to consider avoiding someone who refuses to evolve in this area. You can have too much technology, but none or too little? That can be a disaster waiting to happen.

Quite honestly, I almost did not even include this section because I'm sure there are only so few agents out there who have not embraced technology on some level even if it's through no choice of their own. Good and outstanding agents will still inject "old school" into their systems. "Old school" is not a bad thing. I utilize it, and I would venture to say that most top producers do the exact same thing. Never forget a seller-agent relationship is a human, one-on-one partnership that should have warmth and technology at the same time. Having the proper balance of both is pivotal to a successful real estate transaction. An appropriate amount of "old school" combined with an equally appropriate amount of "technology" is and really should be an ongoing part of this industry.

New Agents

This is a tough one, even for myself. If you are anything like me, you kind of want to help the underdog. You would like to encourage someone who has gone out on a limb to start a new career. But really, for the purposes of hiring an agent, is that your job? I can tell you right now, it is my humble opinion that if you want to successfully sell your home, you should consider eliminating the new agent from the lineup. It could, however, work positively for you; that agent may be so motivated to succeed that you get super service, but there is still a problem, and that is the obvious—you cannot argue it: experience. You may be thinking to yourself, "Hey, Dan, you were a new agent once."

Yes, and I did occasionally get hired early on to represent sellers, and I can honestly say that I did the best I could; however, the truth is that I had to depend on my broker and some other agents to help me throughout the process, and they certainly could not be available 24-7, which is really what I needed.

So, although I appreciated being given the opportunity, and fortunately for my clients, everything ended up okay, in hindsight, to be completely honest and to really try to drive home a point for you, even though I did not know it at the time, those clients really did take quite a risk in hiring me. There is just too much at stake, and quite frankly, I did not get hired that often to be a seller's agent; in many real estate markets throughout the country, generally newbies don't. "Well, then," you may ask, "how in the world does an agent get started in the real estate business?" There are so very many ways. Let's look at just a few of them. But first, please *do not* feel sorry for new agents; they must, as I did, prove themselves like in any profession. Why in the world would a rookie police officer be given the job of a lieutenant straight out of the academy? It makes no sense; hey, that rookie officer still has a job; it's just not as glamorous and neither does it pay as well as a higher-up position. In a market where working with sellers is preferred by agents, new agents may have no other choice than to work with buyers, and even that can be very competitive.

Personally for me, I did just about everything early on in my career, not just working with buyers or occasionally sellers whom many other agents did not want to work with because the price was too low, but I also worked with renters. I would drive prospective tenants around to rental properties and try to get their applications accepted by landlords. It paid very little, but it still paid. I stayed in touch with those tenants, and some eventually became buyers.

I also worked with buyers whom other agents did not want. Perhaps a buyer could not qualify to purchase a home. No problem. I simply put them in touch with a reputable lender who helped them fix credit problems and the like. Sure, it took a while, sometimes even years, but I still stayed in touch. Now who do you think many of those buyers wanted to use once they were qualified? I would also try to do open houses every single weekend; I did whatever I could to build myself a clientele.

How about knocking on doors? Well, you may think agents only do that to get listings, not necessarily. If new agents are so inclined, they could knock on apartment doors to find buyers. Again, those buyers do not have to be qualified, yet anyway. Agents can stay in touch with potential purchasers, help them work on a few things to get themselves in a better position to buy, and then proceed to sell the qualified buyer a home.

One thing I learned very early on was that if agents want to successfully represent sellers, they must know what it is like to represent buyers. That experience will pay you, the seller, huge dividends in the end.

Do not feel bad for new agents; they'll make it. The examples I stated are just a few of the ways they can start their real estate business. So again, new agents? They will prosper—that is, *if* they want to.

Friends and Relatives

I do get this question and in different forms. It can go something like this: "Dan, should I use a friend or relative who is a real estate agent? I mean if I can't trust my own relative, who can I trust?" I'm going to address this very simply, and again, this is just my opinion from observing lots and lots of family/friend transactions:

I DO NOT RECOMMEND IT!

Unless you are willing to take the chance that you may completely sabotage a certain relationship, I would highly urge you not do this to yourself or the other person. But if you really feel that by not using this person you may be also causing damage to the relationship, then here's a great way to get out of it. Find an agent on your own using the methods spelled out in this book and when you are discussing commission, explain the situation to the person about your friend or family member who is a real estate agent, and ask him or her if his or her brokerage would agree to pay your friend or family member's brokerage a reasonable referral fee from their commission when the transaction closes. An outstanding agent may very well agree. This will take some of the ouch away from the whole mess without costing you one dime; As a matter of fact your friend or family member may be quite relieved themselves! Your agent is paying it out of the commission you were going to be paying him or her anyway. I cannot speak for other agents, but in general, I would have no problem agreeing to this.

"I Wear Lots of Hats" Agents

These agents can really get on people nerves, myself included. There's nothing wrong with them; they are certainly not bad or ugly agents. It's just that they seem to spread themselves quite thin. Remember, just like with the newbie agent, I am not saying you should not hire certain agents; rather, I am giving you food for thought.

These agents encapsulate various unrelated services under one umbrella. For example, they may ask: "Do you have a house to sell? I can do it. Do you have commercial property? I can sell it. How about loans? Do you need a loan? What a coincidence! I'm a lender too. You want to buy a home? I'm for sure your person. Oh, your brother owns some land? Great, I happen to be a land sales specialist!"

I think you get my point. Even if these agents really did have all this expertise (which you might seriously want to question), how in the world are they going to properly represent you with all that other stuff going on? Again, this does not mean the agent is bad or ugly, but you just must ask yourself, "Does this person have a tendency of biting off more than one can chew? If so, can that adversely affect me and the results of the sale of my home?" You will note throughout this book that I strongly encourage you to ask lots of questions both to yourself as well as prospective agents.

Bells-and-Whistles Agents

Polar opposites to old-school agents. Unfortunately, you will most likely not recognize these agents until they're at your house at which point you will have become a captive audience in your own home! They will *wow* you with a laundry list of what I call "glitter" or as this section references, "bells and whistles." They will have PowerPoint presentations, virtual slide shows—technology seeping out of their pores—graphs, data, statistics, you name it. I've seen this type in action; they pull every trick out of their hat to try to convince you they're the right one for the job. Now keep in mind, not all bells and whistles are bad; we certainly use them where appropriate, and I know many other top-producing agents do the same, but some agents…I believe perhaps some of them (not all) may just be insecure about their experience. They might not sell that many homes, and so they are overindulging in technology and everything that sparkles and shines to distract and impress you. These are the types of agents I am referring to.

They will probably also have an over-the-top and overly detailed website. That site just has too much and can be counterproductive. It will do everything for you: tell you the weather, show you all sorts of photos that have virtually nothing to do with anything, give you updated non-real-estate-related news, do your grocery shopping for you—the list goes on.

This type of site sometimes includes images of the agents doing things like walking hand in hand with their significant other near a breathtaking body of water or perhaps photos of their children or pets—that's a bit of glitter too, don't you think? Let's address this for a moment, without sounding too insensitive. If I was a homeowner looking at this site, and *I was thinking of selling my home*, I would think to myself, "Nice pics, but truly, why is this person showing this to me? The fact of the matter is that I am facing a very important life-altering change and *I really, really, just want someone who knows what he or she is doing, simple.*"

Truthfully, I'm not sure how the real estate industry got so keen on having agents share their personal lives with the public. I mean in some other professions, like say, for instance, attorneys, doctors, accountants, and so forth, that kind of personalization, as far as I know anyway, is non-existent aside from perhaps some family shots hanging on the office wall.

Can you imagine contacting a lawyer's office for a face-to-face consultation on a very important legal matter only to have the attorney or his or her secretary tell you to first please check out their website and while you are there to also take a look at the family photos from last year's vacation! I'd be a little freaked out, but for some reason the real estate industry kind of went in that direction, and it became a somewhat acceptable practice.

I do believe that it is dying out; that is sharing too much personal immaterial things with prospective clients. I do have my theories on why this became an acceptable practice in the first place. There are simply a lot of real estate agents out there, so much so that for anyone who is not familiar with the real estate industry, it can be tough to distinguish the professionals from the amateurs (another reason I wrote this book, it does not have to be that difficult if you know what to look for; you most certainly can distinguish between the two). I think a lot of agents had to make themselves stand out in a huge crowd and felt that by truly personalizing themselves it could make up for their lack of experience. These agents hope that the customer will relate to their personal life and in doing so hand them their business. Again, this is just my theory, but I do not think I am too far off the mark.

If agents are professional and trustworthy, you will know that from their reputation and experience before you let them into your home, and *then* when you are face to face, you'll find out if you are comfortable with them on a personal level or not.

As I stated earlier, we are all different; some of you may be more drawn to the technical aspect of real estate. I am too! I suppose what I am trying to say is to try to distinguish technology from glitter. Technology, not glitter, is unbelievably important; I've always been on the cutting edge but only to the point that it is applicable and at least somewhat advantageous to my client. In our industry, like all others, you cannot solely depend on technology; if you could, why would you even need a human agent in the first place? Everything could be virtual; think about it. Not all that glitters is gold. Okay, now let's move on to the type of agents I personally feel are the choices picks but not necessarily in the following order.

Choice Picks

Personal Referrals
Great lead, but make sure you ask yourself a question: Who is referring this agent to you? Is it someone who actually used the services of that agent to a successful end? Is it someone whom you admire as well as someone you trust to have good judgment? If so, you have a fantastic lead If on the other hand the person who is doing the referring never even used that agent, is not someone you know that well, or perhaps someone you know but have misgivings about, then consider adding this agent to your interview list, but do be cautious. Also, keep in mind that just because this agent is highly recommended, it does not necessarily mean that this is the right agent for you and your own personal needs.

Farmers
You probably already know this, but for the sake of clarity, in the real estate industry, farmers are agents who, for the most part, list and sell homes in one particular tract or community, sometimes the entire city. These agents plant seeds in the form of mailers, door hangers, cold calls, advertisements, and so forth. They may help a neighborhood hold a community garage sale. They plant and plant and plant in the hope of a good harvest. A lot of would-be farmers go under, as it is very expensive; what if the harvest is bad? Well, no different than a real farmer, they can go belly-up.

I would certainly not discourage you from using the farmer to list your home, but I think it really depends on a number of variables. There is nothing wrong with farming a community of homes, and many of those agents are quite good, even outstanding. That said, I'd like to point out some things you should at least think about.

Can farmers get a little too possessive of their territories? I would say yes, there is a likelihood that could happen; I mean, what farmer would want another farmer planting seeds on his or her land? The difference here is that the real estate farmer does *not* own the land. A potential monopoly like this in your neighborhood or city could end up hurting you.

I personally like to see competition in commerce, and I believe that rings especially true in the real estate industry. I like to know that various agencies are competing for the job of selling someone's home. It pleases me to see different agencies' signs placed in the front yards of houses. I think it keeps agents on their toes and does not allow for the *overconfidence* factor to set in.

Some farmers might start becoming a little too self-assured, and they may not feel the need to give you the service you deserve. Try going to a very popular restaurant, the one that's been there forever and always has a line outside its door—you know the type I'm talking about—almost every neighborhood has one. Now try getting fast and courteous service there. I suspect you may have some challenges in that area. Understand that the owner *thinks* he or she does not have to *wow* the restaurant's patrons anymore. In my opinion this restaurateur is doomed; eventually that artificial confidence is going to result in mistakes. Of course, not all farmers are like this, but this can happen.

One last thought on this subject. Farmers want (really *need*) to be a success in the community; otherwise their reputation can turn for the worse. Success in real estate is the sold/close of transaction factor. These agents want "SOLD" banners on signs and marketing materials, and as fast as possible. Is it costing you money to make a farmer look good? If agents put their own interests over their clients, they are not very good agents, are they? I would even put such agents in the category of "bad." Many farmers I've known are great, but I do want you to keep your eyes open.

Seasoned Agents

This is a wonderful find in the real estate industry, although it has been my experience that such agents are scarce. But make no mistake, they are out there. Just be extra careful; there are ways to convince people that a certain agent is indeed seasoned when he or she is not. Now, for the purposes of this book, a seasoned agent is not necessarily defined as an agent who's been in the industry for a certain period of time. I know agents who have been selling homes for decades whom I would not consider to be anywhere close to seasoned; conversely, I've witnessed agents with around ten years' experience in the industry whom I certainly would recognize to be seasoned.

What makes the difference? Simply the amount of *successful* transactions the agent has had on a very regular basis. The obvious question here is, "Well, how many transactions would graduate a person to be defined as a seasoned agent?" That's a very relative question with relative answers. Much of this may depend on your geographical area, price range, and the market in general. In higher-price-range communities, there can be less homes and more competition, so an agent who sells one to two homes or so a month might be considered seasoned. In some areas where an agent must do more volume to make a living, that agent perhaps would need to sell four or five homes or so per month. What I really want you to understand is that seasoned agents must show a *consistent* amount of sales—year in, year out, bad market, good market, they still produce positive results.

I remember years ago, when I'd only been a few years in the business, I had a client's home that I was chosen to list; the owner was an elderly man who was beginning to show the early signs of dementia, and his daughter interviewed numerous agents for him and ended up picking me. I was delighted as was she. When I called her to confirm our time to get together to sign the listing contract, she apologized profusely saying that her dad's neighbor "knew someone in the business" who evidently had been around a *long* time, so her dad insisted on listing with that person.

I immediately checked on that agent, and yes, he had been in the industry for quite some time. The problem is that he had listed and sold, if memory serves me right, four or five homes, not in the last few months but the last couple of years! If this were my father, I too would want him represented by someone very experienced; I think you would probably share that same sentiment. In this case, longevity in the business was all that the owner needed to hear. My point is this: do not confuse "years" in the business with "amount" of business. There is nothing like regular, consistent, and successful production.

Specialist Agents

I really like these agents, and the best part is that quite often they are also seasoned agents, so you can use them to sell your home even if your sale is not a specialty situation.

With regard to specialty situations, every real estate transaction is different, and the needs are unique. If your home is in foreclosure, you should want to use an agent who is experienced (and if applicable) certified to handle this type of transaction. Divorce? Same thing. Did you inherit a property or were you made a trustee for an estate? Using an agent who specializes in probate and trust sales would be a safer bet. This is also one of the areas in which wearing a different hat is actually a good thing. Understand that wearing different hats is not bad as long as those hats are somewhat within the same general genre. If you do have a situation that needs special attention, you simply cannot beat specialist agents, and again, often they can be absolutely great agents for standard normal sales too.

Past-Experience Agents

If you have an agent you have used to sell your home before and were happy with his or her service then my personal recommendation? Put this book down right now; give it to a friend, or donate it! You're done; you should consider using his or her services again. You already know the agent; the person has already proven his or her ability to you. You don't need someone else. The truth is that most sellers are just not that fortunate—that is, to have a past *successful* relationship with a prior agent. Exceptions to using these agents? Yes, if there is a specialist needed—for instance, you inherited a home or are having foreclosure issues *and* your previous agent does not specialize in that particular facet of real estate—then you really should want to at least interview other agents with that specialty experience before making your final decision.

> So again, these are what I believe to be the choicest picks for you depending on your needs. But now you need to find these agents!

Finding the Best Agent for Your Needs

So there you have it—five great types of prospects for the job of selling your home. Do you necessarily need to find all five? No, not at all. You may not even have a choice; perhaps there is no legitimate farmer in your area, or maybe you do not have an agent you successfully worked with before. Maybe a specialty agent is not necessary. But for the purposes of this book, let's say that indeed you would like to locate all five types of prospects. The past-experience agent is an easy one, but the others? They may take a little digging. Let's address how to find each of them.

Finding the Farmer

You won't have to look very hard for this person's phone number; it's probably on a magnet on your refrigerator or on a calendar hanging in your office. Maybe his or her literature is all over your front porch or maybe even the person's name is tattooed on your forehead! My point is this: this person will not let you forget that he or she is in the real estate business. Again, this *does not* mean this is the right agent to hire, but he or she definitely deserves a chance. Make sure the agent indeed has lots of experience in your area; I've seen "farmers" who spend a huge amount of money on advertisements only to have a handful of sold homes to their names.

How do you know about the farmer's experience? If you see "FOR SALE" and "SOLD" signs in your neighbors' yards and this has been going on for years, then you're good; no other proof of production and track record is needed. If the farmer passes the above test, he or she gets to interview with you. Exceptions? Yes, if you have a specialty sale, make sure the farmer is well versed in that type of sale. You can easily do this by calling them on the phone (don't do this by e-mail) and asking questions. Why not e-mail? (This can apply to any agent, not just the farmer.) Let's say, for example, you have some questions about probate home sales. If you e-mail agents, you give them time to look up information, ask questions from other more experienced agents, and so forth. If you are on the phone, they do not have that luxury. You will know in a matter of minutes if they indeed have the required experience.

Finding an Agent from a Personal Referral

I love referrals, in any aspect of commerce. When someone I know well has had a successful experience with a contractor, doctor, or really anyone in a specialty field, then that is typically the person I choose to at least talk with about their services. Ask people you know and trust, but as we discussed earlier, *only* people you know and trust, if they have an agent they can recommend. If it came from a reliable source and you do not have a specialty issue, this agent is in. Simple. He or she is added to your list.

Finding Specialists

Often you can find these agents by simply asking around; however, I understand it could be uncomfortable asking friends and family about sensitive situations such as foreclosure or divorce. If you are fortunate to have had a farmer or an agent or even a few agents who have been in touch with you for what seems like forever, then ask if they have experience in your particular specialty. Many of these agents are "seasoned," which we will discuss in the next section. Again, and I do not mean to be cynical, just make sure this question is asked on the phone and not via e-mail.

Another way to find these agents is online. Input your needs on a search, and I'm quite confident a lot of agents' names and information will pop up. But be careful: anyone can claim to be anything; look for agents who have credentials, certifications, or some kind of proof that makes you comfortable enough to contact them. We will address online agent searches in more detail in the following section.

Finding Seasoned Agents

This is a very strong contact for you if you are fortunate to have one. They may not be as good as the agent with whom you had a past successful relationship with but are awfully close. These agents are not necessarily farmers, so their literature is not all over your house. So how do you find them? Various methods. If there is a particular agent(s) who for whatever reason has been in touch with you on a regular basis, he or she has great potential to be seasoned. The agent has already proven it to you by ongoing communication. Contact the person. I do not believe it likely that a low-producing agent is going to be calling on you, year in, year out. Chances are he or she would have dropped out of the business already or would have become so discouraged with the production as to have simply lost enthusiasm.

Seasoned agents can be personal referrals too, or they can just come out of the blue. There's an old saying: "When the student is ready, the teacher will appear." I've seen this happen more often than you may think. Joy and I are seasoned agents, and very often people who are looking to sell their home cross paths with us at *the most* appropriate time. If a seasoned agent comes along during the time you are thinking about selling, consider yourself very fortunate; for sure, add the agent to the list of interviewees. You can also search out these types of agents online, but just be careful; some agents are "wannabe" seasoned agents and will describe themselves as such without proper merit. We will address online agent searches in more detail in the following section.

When you are asking questions whether it be by e-mail, phone, or both to self-proclaimed seasoned agents, simply ask them straight out approximately how many homes they list and sell annually, and make sure you are specific; you want to know how many homes they've sold as sellers' representatives. You do not care about how many homes they've sold to a buyer; that is unrelated and can even be counterproductive to your purposes. If you have reasons to doubt their answer about homes listed *and* sold, then that may be a clue that they are not as seasoned as they are leading you to believe. You could ask for some sort of proof in writing, but that can sometimes be an uncomfortable question to ask; really, there is no right or wrong answer to whether or not you should ask. You just have to kind of go with how you feel and how the conversation is going. I would also recommend that you rely on your gut on this, and if you are getting a feeling that they're not being forthright, then it might be a good idea to pass on them. Keep in mind that seasoned agents will talk to you in such a manner that you simply just kind of "know" that they are who they are claiming themselves to be. Exceptions? Yes, if yours is a specialty sale and a seasoned agent does not specialize in what you need, then you have a problem. I will say, however, that I have observed over the years that seasoned agents by the mere fact of their years in the business often do hold many specialties.

Online Agent Searches
As a society we have learned to do just about everything online, and that of course would include finding professionals. Where it pertains to finding a skillful and experienced real estate agent, is this a safe avenue to take? Well, it might be, but you do need to be on guard. There are a number of ways to do a search: you can simply input your personal needs and no doubt you will have many choices in front of you within seconds. Let's take probate, for example; if you input a probate agent search and suddenly you have all these agents claiming to be probate specialists, can you trust that? My answer to this question is this would almost be likened to a personal referral from someone you did not know that well. They refer an agent to you, but does that mean this is the right agent who can be trusted? It could be, and it might be worth at least speaking to the person, but you certainly would not want to limit yourself to just this agent.

Online searches are really no different in my opinion. As a matter of fact, with the personal referral, even though you don't know the person that well, at least there is some semblance of a connection there. Online? Well, you really just don't know. What I would suggest is that you check out these agents' websites and see what kind of proof they have that they truly are who they are representing themselves to be. Do they have any credentials or are they certified in the area you are looking for? If you do not have a specialty situation, are you seeing enough on their site to make you tend to think they are a seasoned agent?

If the agent's sites are making you feel comfortable and you have narrowed down a few agents, then proceed to ask them questions by both e-mail and phone. I recommend starting with an e-mail. When the agents respond, you can pretty much tell by the tone and structure of the e-mail if they really do know what they are talking about. This is also a good way to see how fast an agent gets back to you. If one is slow in responding to an e-mail *before* you are even a client, can you imagine the problems you may have once you are in a contract with the person?

At any rate, if you are satisfied with the e-mail response, then request a callback, so you can talk in person. This is the second test, the phone conversation that is. You should have a pretty good idea of the veracity of an agent's claims just by the way he or she handles the conversation. I suspect that if you, for example, find four or five agents online and use this system, you will probably end up with one or two real estate agents whom you are impressed enough with to invite to the interview.

Now let's address another form of agent online searches, and that is online companies claiming to be able to find you a great agent in your area. Can you trust these companies? My Opinion? Yes and No. I can tell you from experience that I personally worked with a company that was diligent in referring just a few very good agents, myself being one of them. There are, however, companies that will simply sell your information to lots and lots of agents. Now your phone is ringing off the hook, and you are getting all these e-mails from agents wanting to list your home. I'm simplifying things a bit here; there is a lot of gray area with regard to these types of companies, but I just want to give you a working idea of what you need to be aware of.

If you decide to utilize the services of one of these companies, then I would suggest you ask them two questions. First, how do they vet out the agents who will be contacting them so that indeed you are getting quality agents? Second—and this is very important—ask them how many agents will be contacting you. If it's two or three, I would think that acceptable but not more than that. I would personally not want my contact information released to more than three persons no matter what I was searching for.

If you do decide to search for agents online whether its direct to the agent, a referring company or both, just like with anything online, be careful with whom you share your information with. That said, online real estate agent searches could be a wonderful tool for you.

In this chapter I have given you four very good potentials: Typically, the best being the past-experience agent and then seasoned agent, the farmer, the personal referral, and the specialist, not necessarily rated in that order—*and* how to find them.

Let's say, for discussion purposes, that the narrowing-down process yields you three qualified agents...then great! Interview all of them. If you only narrowed down two, that's okay; as a matter of fact, often homeowners find that they are so impressed with one of the agents they narrowed down that they don't even need to interview anyone else; they just know he or she is right for the job. It's both a "feeling" combined with hard facts and experience. This does happen, and it could be an extremely good thing! Why go through an entire interview process if you do not need to?

One last thought: Although this does not seem to happen too much anymore, I have observed that some homeowners can get a little hung up on geographical location of a brokerage. Perhaps back in the pre-Internet days you needed an office that was right in your backyard, but with today's technology, agents have been able to widen their service area. How wide? That's relative to where you live. You may reside in a small farm community, fifty or so miles from the next city; in that case, yes, you might not have any other choice than to use a very local agent. Even if you had an "out of the area" agent whom you wanted to use, my guess is that they might refuse the business; it's just too far. Conversely, if you live in a densely populated area with city upon city on top of each other, then really, do you need an agent with an office right next door to you? I personally do not think so as long as those agents meet proper criteria.

So now you have located and narrowed down a few agents who are fortunate enough to get to interview with you. It is an honor and a privilege for an agent to be invited to the table and one that should not be taken lightly. So be careful who you let in; reread this chapter if you must, but avoid allowing just *any* real estate agent into your home.

"I'm a great believer in luck, and I find the harder I work the more I have of it."

—Thomas Jefferson

3

YOUR PERSONAL NEEDS AND DESIRES

What is it you really need? I have found that homeowners when making the decision to sell their home know exactly what it is they need or desire but quite often just don't know where to start to accomplish that end. This is where having the right agent is crucial. Following are some examples of reasons homeowners (perhaps yourself) may need to sell.

Selling in Order to Purchase another Home
Obviously, this is quite a common reason to sell. This is not a specialty sale, so the specialty agent is not necessary. That does not mean you won't use one of these agents; they have been around long enough and have a variety of clients, many with certain needs, so they had no choice throughout their career than to learn these specialties, but I would say many, if not most of them, certainly do standard sales.

Just understand, in general, this is a very common reason to sell; it will be easier for you to find an agent since what you are doing is again quite common. I would like to add one point: when you are selling *and* buying, obviously the intensity of the transaction doubles. The right agent will help bring that intensity level down a notch or two.

If you are buying in the same area, you may want to consider utilizing the services of the same agent to make things simpler, cleaner, and more proficient. Top-producing agents will most likely have a full-time buyer's agent on their team whom you will be working with on that end—that is, the buying side of the transaction. Or perhaps they will personally represent you in both transactions. Either way is fine as long as they have systems in place.

Conversely, if you are buying outside the area and do not have an agent to represent you in the purchase, then use your listing agent to help you find a like-minded buyer's agent in the area you are moving to.

Inherited Property

Maybe the house was in a trust or perhaps a probate procedure is needed. Whatever the case, this is *for sure* a specialty. Your agent should understand the process and terminology so they can speak intelligently with everyone involved including attorneys. If possible, I'd like to see your potential agent have some sort of schooling or certification in probate and trust sales; perhaps this is a requirement in your particular area—that is, to be certified. Whatever the case, knowledge is power.

Often with inherited properties, there are many persons involved. I have found that it is not uncommon for there to be animosity among them. Let's say, for example, a home has been inherited by three siblings. One sibling has passed away, so now, depending on the situation, that deceased sibling's children may be entitled to a share. The other two siblings never got along with that side of the family, and consequently there has been tension with the nieces and nephews. This sale just got more difficult, didn't it?

Now keep in mind an attorney should be involved in these cases, but that does not mean the agent is not going to have to deal with many of the personality obstacles that come with this type of sale. Let's take it further; perhaps out of those two living siblings, one moved to the other side of the country and has not been involved with Mom or Dad for years. Now we may have a problem between these two. One has been very present in the parents' lives, while the other one just came to visit every five years or so and expected a warm bed and three squares a day and maybe a little spending cash.

This type of thing does happen and truthfully quite often. Sure, the situations can be different, but the bottom line is, that agent had better be well prepared and equipped—he or she, by default, is going to get caught in the cross fire. "Why did you hire that agent?" screams the out-of-state sibling. "Oh, now that money is involved, you're all of a sudden concerned in the affairs of Mom, huh? Where have you been the last twenty-five years!" yells the other. I've heard this in different forms many, many times. Keep in mind, the experienced agent can help simmer things down in situations such as these. In this case, for example, simply conversing with the agent should put the out-of-area sibling at ease. Out-of-area persons in any kind of real estate transaction can feel very vulnerable and rightfully so; the skilled agent knows this and can diffuse their insecurities.

Unfortunately, sometimes there's just no way to avoid the tension and negative results that follow. Joy and I once met with a family; we knew there was tension, so we decided it best to meet in a neutral place. Good thing we did; halfway through our meeting, one of the family members started acting crazy: clenched jaw, aggressive stance—I mean, body-shaking crazy-like. I thought he was going to become violent and so did everyone else including Joy and myself as we sat carefully still and quiet in the hope that things would calm down. Well, they didn't, but thank goodness, eventually angry brother left screaming at the top of his lungs, but no physical damage was done.

So, there we were, left with the rest of a very shaken family. One of them very sheepishly apologized and then asked Joy, "Um, Joy, you didn't by any chance give him a copy of the paperwork, did you? It had my physical address on it, and I may need to put a restraining order on him, and I have been very careful about not letting him know where I live."

Joy was on top of it. "No way," she said. Joy saw the writing on the wall, think we all did. She held that paperwork from angry brother. Why? Because he had no right to it; he was not a party to this particular sale; rather, he was simply a disgruntled brother with whom the others were just trying to make peace. Another agent may very well not have understood the workings of probate and trust sales and may have handed him a copy of the paperwork...that would *not* have been good!

As you can see, inherited property is not only a specialty when it comes to understanding the ins and outs of the logistics involved but also when understanding the ins and outs of the emotions involved.

Attorneys? Of course, almost every one of our inherited-type transaction has an attorney or sometimes multiple ones involved. If a real estate agent does not know how to speak with a lawyer, it can throw fuel on the fire. I personally enjoy working with most attorneys. I find them to be no nonsense and to the point. I typically keep the conversations short, and I always have notes in front of me, so I don't have to call them back because *I forgot to ask them something.* Understand, it could be costing clients every time I have to speak with or even e-mail their lawyer. If an agent is comfortable interacting with attorneys, it will make the real estate transaction all the more smooth and profitable in the end. Yes, there are ways the qualified agent can help you make the transaction a smooth one on many different levels.

Inherited-Property Scenario

An old client of mine called me and said, "Dan, my mother and aunt inherited their mother's (my grandmother's) property. My mom, Kate, is going to handle the sale; would you mind calling her to discuss some things?"

I replied, "Of course, I will call your mom, and thank you so much for referring her to me." I immediately contacted our local title company and had them send me over all the deeds recorded on the house; I did a quick preliminary review of them and was immediately concerned. The property was not in a trust, which meant there could be a probate involved here, and I was not sure how much Kate and her sister knew about probates. I was hoping perhaps they had some information, perhaps paperwork or better yet an attorney who could shed some light on their situation.

Now I knew where this house was, and I knew the neighborhood quite well: extremely high-end, hugely in demand. This property would sell fast and probably have multiple offers. I called Kate; she thanked me for contacting her, and I proceeded to set up an appointment for Joy to meet with her and her sister. I wanted to ask her some follow-up questions regarding the title, a trust, probate, whether she had an attorney or not, and so forth, but she sounded extremely rushed, and it was clearly obvious she needed to get off the phone as soon as possible. I already knew the mother had passed on and that this was an inherited property; therefore I opted to just let Joy address all those questions at their appointment. I will let Joy take it from here…

I arrived at the property well before our appointment. This is normal for me because I like to get some ground work done prior to meeting with the client. I saw that the property was in average condition. I was not sure how long ago their mom had passed away, but the house looked relatively well kept.

When I went to the door, both sisters answered and introduced themselves to me. Kate, who is the one evidently handling everything with regard to their late mother's estate, seemed a bit hurried and scattered, while her sister, Anne, was quite the opposite, very timid and subdued. After I went through the house, we all sat down, and I proceeded to tell them how sorry I was about their mom. Kate said, "Thank you, I appreciate that; the doctors say they are not sure how much longer she has to live, probably a few months."

Huh? I thought. "Their mother is alive?" Although I was glad their mom had not passed, Dan told me her son said they'd inherited the property. Well, evidently not.

Now usually Dan is very good about having all his ducks in a row before I go out to an appointment, but he did explain the situation and felt it best for me to ask them questions at my appointment since we already knew this was an inherited property. I admit I was caught off guard; in addition there were now new concerns I had based on getting this information about their mother not being deceased.

I decided to go in a different direction and proceeded to ask questions about their mom: how many children she has, what she did for a living, and so forth. I am always sincerely interested in knowing about the person who owned (or in this case owns) the property. Probate and trust sales (although this was not one at this juncture) aside from being a bit technical on the logistics end are also a very emotionally charged transaction especially when it comes to families and, in this case, siblings. Getting them to talk about their mother I knew would help maybe slow Kate down a little, and again, I really was interested to hear about their mom.

Kate lightened up a bit after we got talking, but her sister Anne started tearing up. Kate went on to tell me that her mom is never coming home and that she and Anne have decided to sell the property; they wanted it sold as soon as possible and were hoping I could get it on the market this upcoming weekend. Kate had a power of attorney to sign, which she showed me. I asked her if her Mom had an attorney; Anne was quiet, and Kate said no. She then proceeded to tell me again that her mom only had a few months more to live and that they wanted this property sold *and* closed escrow before that happened. Kate was *extremely* anxious to get this done and fast.

I am not an attorney nor am I tax professional and I would never even begin to pretend that I am. As a matter of fact, let me say right here and now, do not take legal and tax advice from anyone who is not a professional in that area and that includes your real estate agent. Even if they are certain they are right in what they are telling you, it is inappropriate to move in that direction without consulting with the proper professional.

That said, sometimes by the mere fact that a real estate agent is seasoned, he or she can often sometimes see things that look *off* or can even just get a gut feeling that a situation is not right. This was most certainly one of those cases. I said, "Kate and Anne, I really think you should see an attorney as soon as possible." Kate said she had no time, she was only here for a week and needed to fly back home. She needed to get this house on the market as soon as possible. I told her, "I'm sorry, Kate. I just don't feel comfortable listing this property unless you speak with an attorney."

Kate then proceeded to tell me, "Joy, I know this is a very high-end home; you and Dan came to me very well recommended, which is why I want to work with you, but I do have a friend in the business, and she called me just last night and said she would be more than happy to list this property and put it on the market in the next couple of days. She certainly did not see any problems and said nothing about an attorney." Kate admitted her friend was a part-time agent.

I told her, "Look, Kate, I very much want to be your agent, and I know this is a tough time for you and your family, but I just do not feel comfortable moving forward and having anyone sign anything at this juncture; I really urge you to speak to a professional."

She paused for a little, and then Anne chimed in, really for the first time since I had gotten there. "Well, Kate, you know I have been taking care of Mom now for over ten years; I know you are rushed and have to get back to work and all, but I don't think a few extra days is going to make any difference. As a matter of fact, I still have to find a place to live, you know!"

I felt some friction when I'd gotten there, but now it had escalated; this was nothing new for me. Kate was silent and then said, "Okay, Joy, just so I understand, you can't work with us?"

"No, I can, and I will work with you; I want very much to do so. However, both Dan and I have some concerns about you selling this property without legal council." Kate paused again, lightened up a little, looked at Anne and then at me, and said, "Fine, if it's that important to you, Joy, I will take your advice."

A few days later, I received a call from a gentleman with a very demanding voice. *"Joy, please."*

"Yes, this is she."

He said, "Attorney Williams here. I just got finished meeting with Kate regarding her mother's home; I'm sure you are familiar with it?"

"Yes, of course, I am," I said.

He went on. "Joy, do you have *any* idea what would have happened had you listed and sold this property without Kate and Anne speaking to me first?"

"Well, yes," I said, "both my partner and myself had somewhat of an idea, so I was very adamant about her seeking legal council."

He continued, "Had she not met with me and if you'd sold that property, the financial liability on the family would have been in a word, *catastrophic*. Great job, Joy; I'll be in touch."

Kate called me soon thereafter, apologized, and thanked me profusely for my stubbornness in not agreeing to list the property. She told me she'd decided to take some time off work and stay with Anne for the next couple of months to help out and that in the meantime her lawyer would be in touch with me. A few months later Mr. Williams did call me; he told me that Kate and Anne's mother had passed away but that all proper paperwork was now in order so to please move forward with the sale of the property.

Inherited-property sales can take on a much different light than your average standard sale; there are emotions involved, family tension, and certain legal issues that should be addressed and reviewed by the proper professionals. If you have inherited a property, make sure your agent understands the ins and outs when it comes to probate and trust sales. Choose your agent well, extremely well.

Foreclosure

I am going to basically mirror this to the above inherited-property section with regard to emotions and personalities. However, there could be more at stake for the homeowner. A property in foreclosure is literally being threatened by a legal process. If agents do not know what they are doing, people could *lose their homes.* I cannot be emphatic enough as to the importance of experience. As with trust and probate, schooling and certification, if applicable or required, or even if it is not, it sure could help.

Foreclosure is a tough one. Agents might be dealing with homeowners who may have a perceived feeling of failure. I say "perceived" because often the homeowners are not at fault, at least not at the level some of them think they are. They may have gotten caught up in a bull market only to find the purchase was at the very peak and it had all gone downhill from there. Perhaps money was borrowed on the house for very good reason: illness, business startup, schooling, whatever the case. These persons can often be in a very emotionally and financially vulnerable position.

Now remember, there is a legal process going on, and lenders want their money back—simple. They do not really care about the loss of job, illness, and so forth; all they know is that they and their investors are in a financial situation that requires a fix. Well, it could, among other things, be some kind of loan modification, or of course, it could be simply taking the house back or auctioning it off. Now in order to really help homeowners, knowing how to deal with these lenders is absolutely essential.

Let's say a lender is for sure going to foreclose. If agents go in there too passively, they may get walked on. Too aggressive? They can get stomped. There is a way in which to deal with lenders and a way not to. If dealt with properly, agents can help lenders see that perhaps foreclosing on their mutual clients is not the best financial move for them, the lenders, that is.

It is very common to run into brick walls with persons in the foreclosure and collection departments. I can pretty much prove to them that foreclosing on our client will end up hurting the lender and their investors in the end, but to no avail. What do I do when I hit a brick wall? I will usually go over the persons' heads, sometimes *way* over, perhaps in the form of a certified or registered letter.

Now often the person is so high up that he or she will never receive my letter, but you can pretty much bet that someone will. Letters like these, if they are sent properly, are almost always opened, in my experience. The person who does end up opening and reading these types of correspondence is often the gatekeeper, someone hired to keep things as easy on the higher-up as possible, not getting pestered by a real estate agent being one of them. These gatekeepers aside from protecting their boss, also want to protect the company and the shareholders and can sometimes better make sense of what I was trying to convey to the person I was initially working with. If you or anyone you know is in foreclosure, make darn sure the agent has the capacity and wherewithal to handle dealing with both small and large lending institutions.

So, there it is: very similar to inherited property but with the addition of a legal foreclosure system threatening property. I will say, however, I have had many situations that had both things going on at the same time. Not only was the property in probate, for example, but also it was being foreclosed on. This is where agents with multiple specialties are worth their weight in gold. The right agent for the job is out there, and with the tools in this book, you can find that person and take advantage of his or her expertise.

Short Sales

I am sure you have heard the term before, but if not, allow me to briefly explain what a short sale is. I'll use a simplified example. Let's say a home is worth $400,000, but a buyer paid $600,000 for it a few years back when the market had reached a peak. That buyer was given a loan to purchase the home in the amount of $540,000; the buyer put up 10 percent, in this case, $60,000, as down payment. Recap: $540,000 loan plus $60,000 cash down payment from buyer for a total of $600,000, the purchase price of the home.

Down the road, this buyer, who of course is now the owner, perhaps fell into some financial difficulties and needs to sell but cannot. Too much is owed; it would be considered being "upside down." The person simply owes more than the home is worth. In this case, let's say the loan balance is down to $500,000. Now what? It is highly unlikely that the owner with a financial hardship can make up the difference of $100,000 plus closing costs and commissions; as a matter of fact, he or she probably cannot even make the monthly payments. And let's not forget, this person has already lost their $60,000 down payment to begin with!

Well, this is a real estate sale that will simply be short of enough money to close escrow, thus the term "short sale." In this case, the shortage amount is again in the range of about $125,000 between the difference in value versus the loan, commissions, escrow fees, property taxes, and so forth. Where does that $125,000 come from? It can come from the lenders who are holding the note on the property by them taking a lower amount than what is owed. The process can become very difficult, much more so for the agent than the homeowner. With the right agent who is experienced in this sort of thing, The homeowner will typically need to do very little. The person will have given the agent the authorization to deal with the lender on his or her behalf.

I've been helping homeowners with short sales for decades; they are not easy and can be very complicated, but if done properly they have a decent likelihood of getting approved. That's right, you need to get approval for a short sale. Lenders are certainly not going to, in essence, hand over

$125,000 without doing their own due diligence. They want to know what happened. Why can the homeowner no longer keep this property? Is $400,000 really what this home is worth? They are not going to take yours or your agent's word for this kind of thing; there is a lot of money at stake, and investors are not happy about it; at the same time, if they foreclose on the property that could (but not always) end up costing them much more than the $125,000 they would lose in a short-sale situation.

If the consensus is that a short sale is the best option, then use the tactics spelled out in this book to find that qualified agent. Short sales are actually one of my favorite types of sales because I am challenged by it and I really do know what I am doing. I've dealt with some situations where there were multiple lenders on the property, not just one. In addition, there were liens, back taxes, city assessments, and so forth. I have still been able to make such short sales work, save my clients from foreclosure, and in most cases, get them some relocation money to help with their move. It gives me pleasure to know that I truly helped these clients. Make sure your agent is very well qualified and preferably certified in short sales, which may even be a requirement in your area. You have a lot at stake, and always speak to an attorney and a tax person. Find out what is the best course of action for your personal situation.

Short-Sale Scenario
Victor and Carol had purchased their home years ago when the prices were much lower. However, after the values had appreciated substantially, they decided to take a second loan on the property to start a new business and to help their children with college. Well, the college part went great, but the business…not so much. They ended up getting well behind in payments, forcing the lender to start foreclosure. When I first spoke with Victor and Carol, they both told me they did not want to sell the property but rather were working with the lender on a loan modification. I told them what I tell many of my clients in that position. "Great job, and make sure to be very communicative with your lender throughout that modification process; lenders generally like prompt communication from their borrower."

I hate to see anyone lose their home, and if there is a chance to successfully keep it, I'm always in support of that; how could anyone not be? I also told them to make sure they have legal representation on an appropriate level. Well, that modification review went on for some time, but we still stayed in touch. I repeatedly told them that if for whatever reason the modification fell through to let me know immediately and that we could always try to do a short sale on the property. The house was way upside down; they owed much more than what it was worth.

I made sure they understood that the short sale was only a last resort, only if everything else failed. I just wanted them to know there was some kind of safety net or option they might be able to take advantage of other than foreclosure, again only if there were no other choices left. They thanked me, and even more time went by, a few months actually, and then I got the call. "Great news, Dan; we got the modification!" I was happy, very happy for them. They went on to tell me that the lender said this was a trial thing and that if even one payment were missed that would cancel the terms of the modification.

I encouraged them to stay positive and just do the best they could, and I continued to stay in touch with them. About six or so months went by, and I got another call; this was not a jubilant one. Something had happened, and Victor and Carol just could not make another payment. The modification was canceled, and foreclosure proceedings went into effect. I asked them if they wanted to do the short sale, and to my surprise, they said no. I asked why, and they said they'd found another entity with a program that might help them. I supported them both completely but also told them to be very careful and to not let the property foreclose from under them. They thanked me, agreed, and promised they would stay in touch. They kept that promise. Now keep in mind, when I initially spoke with Victor and Carol, I advised them to seek legal and tax counsel. They were good about that and did have someone helping them and advising them from a legal and tax standpoint.

I told them that if this new entity did not work out for them and the appropriate professionals advised a short sale, I would be there for them.

They knew I was certified in this type of sale—short sales, that is—and assured me I was the one with whom they would work with should that happen. About a month later Carol called and told me their attorney said it was a lost cause and to do the short sale and to try avoid getting a foreclosure on their record; their accountant agreed.

Joy met with both of them, and we started the process; however, it had many more complications than I was aware of. They actually had three loans on the property. In addition the property taxes had not been kept up and neither were the association dues in the community they lived in. Further, they had some other legal problems stemming from the failed business that had resulted in liens being placed on their home. No short sales are easy for an agent to do even under the best of circumstances, but this one…highly complex.

I told them both I was up to the job and very confident I could help. (Here again, note how powerful sincere confidence is in an agent! It really does help put the client's mind at ease.) When I spoke to their main lender, the one foreclosing on them, I explained both verbally and in writing that their patience in not foreclosing would actually benefit them financially much more than going through with the foreclosure.

They postponed the auction date numerous times on my request, but on the last postponement, it was certainly not without a fight. I ended up having to go pretty far up to find someone who would be receptive. I did this with hard proof in the form of a package at least fifty pages thick; again they postponed. It took a while, but I got everyone on board: the other two lenders, the lienholders, the association, everyone. They all cooperated partly because I was able to, in different ways, convey the following to all the involved parties: "A little of something is better than a whole lot of nothing." Everyone settled.

We closed the short sale, and Victor and Carol moved into an apartment using the relocation funds I got for them as part of the short-sale deal I negotiated. I kept in touch with them, and from our conversations, I could tell they were actually doing better than ever. For one, the pressure of the house and all those liens and taxes against them were off. With that freed-up energy, they performed some major due diligence and, as a result, found a private investor to back them on another business venture and this time…a success! What was better, for Victor and Carol anyway, the real estate market had hit a pretty big dip, and now they were in a position to buy their own home back (not literally their home but one similar, actually better) at a much lower price. Because their attorney advised them to avoid a foreclosure, they were able to qualify for a home loan sooner than later.

What seemed to be a devastating period of time for Victor and Carol had a happy ending. They felt they were back in the game and feeling great. I'm glad I wear that "short sale hat"; it has proven to be one of the more rewarding aspects of my job.

Foreclosure with Equity (No Short Sale Necessary)

This happens frequently especially in a strong market. A property is in foreclosure, but there is no need for a short sale. Why? Because there is no shortage here; there is still equity in the property. In other words, based on the current value of that home there is enough money to pay the lender(s), commission, closing costs, and so on and still have money left over for the homeowner. Let's use the same example we did for the short sale, but in this situation the property is worth $600,000, and $500,000 is owed. So there is a gross amount of $100,000, and after all the amount owed and costs…well, a still very sizeable check for the homeowner whose other option might have been losing the home to foreclosure.

Warning! Be very careful if you are in foreclosure; unscrupulous persons, among other things, may try to convince you that you have little or no equity (money) in the property when in fact you do. Contact a reputable agent to give you a true value on your home before making any decisions. You can even hire a certified appraiser to appraise your home, if there is any doubt as to what the home is worth. If there was ever a time to have an accurate and realistic estimate on your home's value, it is in these type of transactions. There is a time clock, and proper pricing for a fast but still profitable sale is crucial. Take no chances on losing your equity.

I have heard homeowners say this to me many times, "But they're auctioning my home off in two weeks; there is not enough time!"

My response: "Not necessarily." Especially if the lenders are going to get all their money in full, they may postpone that foreclosure sale for you, but to do that, they ordinarily need to see some written reassurance that they will indeed get paid—for instance, an offer on the property, a listing contract, paperwork from escrow, a good-faith estimate proving they will get a full payoff, and so forth. I have found that if the agent or attorney for the client, if applicable, presents a complete and orderly package to the lenders basically proving that they, the lenders, will get paid, they frequently go ahead and postpone that sale to give the process enough time to close.

If you are in a foreclosure situation where there is equity involved, you have options, I would urge you strongly to talk to a legal and tax professional and again, to keep in touch with your lender; as long as you communicate with them, the odds of them working with you increase dramatically.

Foreclosure Scenario with Equity (No Short Sale Necessary)

Janet was referred to me by a past client. Her home was well into foreclosure by the time I was introduced to her. She said she only had about a month before they could take the property back and thanked me for calling but that there was not much I can do. She went on to tell me her place needed a lot of work and she knew selling homes could take some time and there simply was not enough—time, that is. I did what I almost always do and told Janet that I need to do a little investigating but that I would get back to her immediately. I ran her address and saw that she owned a condo. I knew this complex quite well, and I also know that these condos were government approved for loans and sold very fast.

I checked the title company and found that everything was in order. She only had one loan on the property and no liens, and I knew that I would be able to get about $400,000 for the unit. I could also see in the foreclosure papers that were recorded on the property that indeed Janet was right; as a matter of fact she had less time that she thought, a little under three weeks before they could foreclose. I also noted that the amount owed on the property including all the back payments was about $275,000.

I phoned Janet and told her I wanted Joy to meet with her as soon as possible, like tomorrow. When Joy arrived at the unit, she could see that it was indeed in pretty bad shape, but it had one of the better locations in the complex. Joy figured its value in an "as is" condition and to sell fast to be in the range of about $375,000. Joy went on to ask Janet if she was behind on her association dues also?

She said, "No, not at all" and that she was only behind on her mortgage. We felt she could easily get about $70,000 (net check to Janet) give or take if we sold the property for around $375,000. Janet, although pleased to hear that, went on to tell Joy that there was just not enough time. Joy reassured her that was not necessarily true. Joy commented and continued to explain to her that if we got an offer fast enough on the property I could explain the situation to the lender and with proper documentation probably get the lender to postpone the foreclosure sale. Janet said that, well, another person, not a real estate agent, had come to her door a few nights ago and told her that if she deeded the property to him that he would hand her a cashier's check for $15,000. Janet said this person said he would deal with the lender.

Now let me share what I think this person was going to do. I knew from the foreclosure papers that Janet was not that behind, monetarily I mean. Yes, she was almost a year behind in payments, but those monthly payments were really not that much; she had a low interest rate, and all told, she owed about $20,000 to the lender in back payments. Now remember, her association dues were current as were her property taxes. So, this person was going to have Janet deed the house to him, and he was, in exchange, going to give her $15,000. Once that happened my suspicion was that he was going to contact the lender and pay them the $20,000, bringing the loan current and out of foreclosure. So, he would be into this transaction for $35,000. He was then likely to spend another $20,000 or so fixing the place up and then because of its great location sell it for at least $425,000. A total net after commissions, closing costs, really everything, of over $80,000 (net check to investor).

Janet was basically handing over a huge amount of *her* equity to this buyer by deeding over her property. Even after Joy explained this to her, she was hesitant; why? A variety of reasons…for one, doubt that we could get the foreclosure postponed, which was a reasonable concern, and also she saw that $15,000 being waved in her face. Should she take the $15,000 or are there other options? As we do with all clients, we strongly recommended her seeking legal advice and fast. Joy did not push the issue of us listing and selling the property, as Janet was clearly undecided as to what to do. Joy just told her to talk to an attorney and that she could come back tomorrow night, if necessary. (Remember, we had very little time; every day was crucial.)

I will hand it to Janet; she contacted her attorney the very next morning. He advised her to move forward listing the home with us; he happened to know our reputation and told her the odds were quite strong the foreclosure would be postponed. "However," said the attorney, "I want to be very clear that there is no guarantee of that, so there is some risk." It was basically getting $15,000 now for sure or a very high probability of getting about $65,000 later. Janet chose the latter, we got a little more for the unit than we expected, and she netted about $70,000.

Now, would it have been a mistake if Janet had chosen the other route instead? Absolutely not. As long as her attorney was watching over the transfer, I would have completely understood. In the end, although I was very confident, there was no guarantee I could get that foreclosure postponed; we were very up front with both Janet and her attorney about that.

Sometimes in foreclosure situations like this, it is very tough knowing what to do. If you or anyone you know are in this position, then it is my suggestion to find out what the home is worth by a reputable real estate agent(s) and perhaps an appraiser and subsequently find out how much equity is in the property (i.e., net, after all the costs) and that most importantly, to seek legal council. This is a very strong combination: knowing the true value, an estimate on the net, and legal advice. In this case, that combination turned out to be a very positive financial move for Janet.

Divorce

This is a very tough one, and if you are reading this book, and divorce is what is forcing your home to be sold, then let me first say how sorry I am.

Divorce and moving are two very emotionally exhausting experiences; you are having to go through both at the same time. Inherited property and foreclosure may have emotions tied in with them, but divorce...emotions on steroids, in my opinion.

Is divorce a specialty sale like probate or inheritance? You bet. If you are fortunate to know of an agent (and I would recommend someone neither of you know on a personal level) who has divorce-sale experience, then you are way ahead of the hiring process. But keep in mind, and this is extremely important: agents who handle a divorce sale must understand that their job is to sell the house, *not* to take a certain position with either of the parties. Many agents obstruct their better judgment by giving into a tendency to take sides. *This is wrong.* An outstanding agent would never let that tendency get in the way of representing both parties in a neutral, equal, and professional manner; I feel very strongly about this. This is one of the reasons why I recommended avoiding an agent you know personally.

Now here we are dealing with a legal system in a different way. I have found that inherited property and foreclosure scenarios are often (but not always) a bit cut and dry. But divorce...often in and out of court can seem more the norm. Here is a situation as an example, where an agent has listed a property, but then a month or so into the listing and marketing, one party decides not to sell. Perhaps, they are trying to work things out and not get a divorce, which of course I would personally be completely in support of, but it can also be a ploy to rattle the other person. Perhaps, the longer the house is on the market, the more it is costing one of the spouses money, sometimes literally out of his or her pocket. Sure, they can take that to the judge, but that costs money too. Divorce sales can get very ugly and expensive, and some can seem to go on indefinitely.

The wrong agents can make things worse; perhaps they are getting frustrated because they feel as though they are putting too much time into it and want to close this escrow and get paid and fast. Here's the thing, in my opinion: the agent's clients are in crisis whether the clients know it or not. For Mr. or Ms. Real Estate Agent to get a bad attitude toward Mr. and Mrs. Divorce can be very inappropriate. That agent knew, or should have known, what he or she was getting into with this listing and should have been prepared for it.

Here is where skilled agents will also be able to make the buyer's agent more comfortable and thus help keep the buyer from bailing on the deal. If applicable, they can also work closely with the attorneys involved and help the mutual clients make sense of certain situations where it pertains to the sale of the home.

Again, if you are reading this and personally going through a divorce, all I can say is I'm sorry, and I really hope you follow the guidelines in this book; if ever you needed a patient, competent, and professional agent, it is now. Joy mostly handled the following scenario; this is a great example of what I am referring to.

Divorce Scenario
Ted's and Rachel's attorneys contacted Dan and asked him to set up an appointment for me to meet with both of them. The attorneys said it was best he speak directly with Rachel to make the appointment at this juncture. Dan did as he was requested. One of the questions he asks clients who are going through a divorce is this: "Would you like Joy to meet with you together or separately?" In many cases the two are not on speaking terms and cannot be in the same room with each other. This was one of them. Rachel thought I should meet with her first since she is the one living at the property with their two small children; everyone agreed. As a professional I do not get emotionally involved with my clients, but I am very sensitive to the emotions they are feeling. My job is to list and sell the property for the best price possible to help the client and the courts move forward with the divorce proceedings. Yet, I cannot help but feel empathy for all parties involved in a divorce.

Rachel was nice enough, not very talkative, pretty much to the point and kept our meeting brief; this is not unusual, that is, for homeowners going through a divorce to not want to spend any more time than necessary with a real estate agent. After I secured her signatures on everything, I proceeded to contact Ted. He was, of course, very serious on the phone; we made an appointment for him to come to the office to also sign. When I met with him, I would not say he was pleasant or unpleasant, rather unemotional and somewhat detached. Since I had already seen his home,

I had an idea what the fair market value should be; both attorneys and Ted and Rachel all agreed with me on the price. Ted, however, decided to change his mind and told me so at our meeting. The result? I could not move forward. I contacted the attorneys and let them know what was happening; they said they would get back to me.

Well, that took about a month. What had evidently happened is that they'd both gone back to court for a few different matters including the pricing of the house. They agreed to go with a higher price, not as high as Ted wanted, but still too inflated in my professional opinion. I did as instructed and moved forward. I met with Rachel again and then with Ted and got everything properly signed with the new price; however, Ted said he did not want any agents showing the property for at least another month. Rachel agreed, the attorneys agreed, and we held off. A month went by, and Rachel called me and said they were both ready to go on the market, but Ted wanted no sign in the yard and also said that we could only show the property during the mornings midweek. Well, being pretty much a weekend business, I knew that would be a big problem, but I proceeded as directed and kept both attorneys in the loop.

Another month went by; there was no activity, which was not a surprise to any of us. The house was overpriced, not in great shape, and nearly impossible to show. It was around this time that Rachel called me, very upset, and almost in tears, she said she did not want to tell me but that they were facing serious financial problems and had not made a payment in nearly four months. This was very concerning to me but fortunately the lender had not started foreclosure. I thanked her for being candid but told her that we had to let the attorneys know immediately. She said they'd already done so. I told both of them and their attorneys that if the lender started foreclosure, then it would become public information and that would hugely decrease their leverage; buyers might think them desperate. Rachel was concerned; Ted did not seem to care.

I was told to continue to market the property at that same price and that agents could still only get in the house during midweek mornings. I proceeded but was very up front with everyone involved about my concerns. By the way, this is a good time to bring up another point about agents who work with divorce-related real estate sales. For the most part, I feel e-mail is a preferred mode of communication because everyone is copied on everything, and there is full transparency.

Sure enough, the lender started foreclosure. I immediately went to all four parties and told them that I was now extremely concerned. In addition, even though they had borrowed a lot of money on the house, there was at least $50,000 equity in the property that was now being threatened by a legal system. The attorneys agreed with my concerns as did Rachel, but Ted…that did not seem to phase him. He told me, "Joy, they can just foreclose on the property." I explained to him the dangers and repercussions of that and what could be lost; he kind of just shrugged his shoulders. I must tell you that during this process, I got to know Ted a little better; he was actually very polite, firm but polite and kind of soft spoken. On some occasions he would tell me about how happy he was when they'd originally purchased the property but that a few years ago he had had an accident and lost his job. He told me he was not always like this. Ted did not care anymore; that was obvious.

From what I could gather from having sold many, many homes that were the result of a divorce was that Ted's emotions were getting in the way of him making rational and well-thought-out decisions. Ted was a good father, and Rachel, a good mother; that seemed obvious enough, yet Ted was willing to see $50,000 lost—that money, of course, could go to the children's care, education, and so on. I do not think he was being vindictive, but rather, he was letting his emotions blind him. In addition, it was painfully obvious that Ted was procrastinating the sale of the home; he simply did not want to face or deal with it. I contacted all parties on a conference call: Ted, Rachel, and their respective attorneys. I told them we needed to reduce the price and get agents in there on weekends. Everyone agreed, but Ted. That meant the attorneys would have to make another court date to get a judge involved; we just did not have much time. It was then that I completely realized that no matter what I said, he was not going to see this from my point of view or from anyone else's for that matter. I then, on that conference call, asked permission to meet with Rachel and Ted alone at the house; I was adamant, not my office but the house.

Remember, these two did not want to be in the same room together, so I was not sure how this would be received, but I was running out of options; the foreclosure time clock was ticking, and I had a responsibility to get this home sold.

To my amazement Ted jumped on it and said sure. When?" I think we were all surprised, including Rachel. All parties agreed with the meeting, so we met at the house, just the three of us; the children were not there. I let them start talking about things other than real estate; I mostly listened. They talked about their kids and how proud they both were of them. I then slowly brought up the discussion of the house but not with regard to selling it, rather about when they'd purchased the property. I asked what their real estate agent was like, and so forth.

Ted suddenly lightened up. He smiled for the first time that I'd met him and started going on about the yard and what a mess it was and how he'd cleaned it up and put up a swing set for the kids, and so forth. I could tell Ted was sad, but he was also much more relaxed; he and Rachel even made some jokes. Now I have known people in my life on a personal level who had lost a spouse through death; some of them could not even fathom looking at a photo of happier days gone by, but others? They relished it; it made them feel good to see those photos. Ted was one of these types; the memories brought him some semblance of peace. My hunch worked. I had a feeling that if I got them both in the house together in a relaxed noncourtroom atmosphere there might be a change in direction. Ted finally apologized to me and to a shocked Rachel and told me to reduce the price and let agents come anytime they want.

For whatever reason, Ted just needed to be reminded of something good, as he had been surrounded by nothing but negativity for years, well, evidently since his injury. We were not quite out of the woods yet, however. A week or so later, the attorneys called me and said there was a new dispute with regard to the equity split and neither of them would agree to an offer until this was resolved. I told the attorneys that while I understood, it would be my strong advice to still move forward, sell the property, and close escrow since the house was in foreclosure and perhaps the attorneys could simply place the funds from the sale in a trust where it would remain until such time as when they made an agreement.

The attorneys were thinking on those same lines. Ted and Rachel were both on board with that. We soon thereafter received a good offer on the property and proceeded to close the transaction. Dan continued his follow-up and checked in with both of them over the years. He found out that over time Ted and Rachel actually became very close and shared in many of the children's activities together.

Divorce is sad; there is no doubt about that, and just about every emotion out there can surface during the process. This was a perfect example of how some of those emotions could have had a hand at bringing more economic stresses to Ted, Rachel, and their children. This scenario could have been the other way around; I have seen many different variations of this. It could have been Rachel that was the difficult one or in many cases both of them. The bottom line is that although I do not get emotionally involved in divorce-related sales or any type of sale really, I can still observe those emotions, be empathetic and supportive, and discern if any of them, emotions that is, are getting in the way of what both parties hired me to do; this was a perfect example.

Investment Property

Let's say you own an investment property, and you have decided to sell. Is this a specialty? Yes, I think so, but perhaps not to the same degree as the aforementioned challenges. Investment property often means tenants; tenants, in general, are not happy campers after they discover they have to move. We had one particular transaction wherein the tenants had been in the property for decades with no rental agreement and very low rent. It was a multiunit piece of property. So, three individual tenants none of whom showed anything but distaste toward everyone involved in this. This was also a trust sale, which can have its own complications; this is a perfect example of the power of an agent who has multiple specialties but in the same general genre. Bottom line is if we did not have experience with how to deal with tenants on a personal one-on-one level as well as probate/trust experience, that transaction would have been an absolute nightmare for the homeowner.

Investment property can have other challenges. Often the property is or becomes vacant. That can pose a variety of different problems that must be addressed. Your investment can be, in a sense, a sitting duck for the wrong people or simply the elements. Yes, vacant properties can have obstacles, and having an agent who can guide you on how to avoid or at least limit those problems is very valuable. Try to find a real estate agent with experience in this type sale. And yes, speak to your legal and tax people with regard to the sale of investment property.

Investment-Property Scenario

I received a call from the owner of a rental property here in Southern California. His name was Roy, and he lived out of state and had decided to sell the property. He told me he had spoken to a tax consultant, who agreed with the sale of the property.

As a matter of fact, he was going to do an exchange into a property closer to where he lived. He asked if we had experience with exchanges, to which I told him, "Yes, we have been involved with many over the years and understand the logistics involved as does the escrow and title company we work with." I went on to ask him if he had located a replacement property; he told me he had no agent yet. I advised him that I would take care of that for him and find him a reputable agent in his area who was also familiar with exchanges.

We went on to talk about his home out here. He said he had had the same tenant in there for well over twenty years, and he had only raised the rent twice during that entire time, and he was aware he could have been getting a much higher amount. I knew because of that low rent there could be trouble ahead.

Joy and I have a system with rental-property sales that we follow, and part of that system pertains to dealing with the occupant. I asked if his tenant would be cooperative. Roy said, "Well, he had better darn be with the rent I've been charging him." Sometimes the most difficult tenants are the ones who have been getting a great deal; the obvious reluctance of having to relocate into a higher rental bracket propels most of that difficulty. I asked Roy if he had told the tenant that he was going to sell. He said, "Yes, his name is Jim, and he'll be expecting your call." Now this is something I always leave to the homeowner; sometimes they want us to take care of letting the tenant know the property will be sold, and other times, they prefer us to do it. We are fine with either way.

One of the first things we do when selling rental properties is to get the listing contract signed by the homeowner. We want to have that with us when we meet with the tenant. Seeing a contract puts more of a reality into the tenant's mind that indeed this has to happen. If after we get into the property, we see that it is in worse or better shape than we thought, we can always recommend our client to adjust the price up or down at a later time. For now, it's important we have that contract with the owner, so we can start the wheels turning.

Roy complied as we requested, and I proceeded to call the tenant to make an appointment for Joy to meet with him and take a look at the property. I left him a message, no response. Another, no response. I left one more message, and still nothing. I contacted Roy. He was none too happy. Understand, we will usually call the tenant for our client where appropriate, but sometimes, as in this case, we simply have no other choice than to have the owner contact their tenant directly. At any rate, Roy told me, "I can't believe he is not returning your calls, Dan; I apologize. Let me call him." A few days later, Roy called me back. He said even *he* had a hard time getting hold of him but that he eventually did. He told me the tenant, although not happy about having to move, would cooperate and meet with us.

When I called, he answered this time. I introduced myself and told him I had been hired to sell the property. I am always extremely friendly and nonthreatening in my tone of voice with tenants. After I introduce myself in these scenarios, I will typically stay silent for a moment and wait for the reaction. The response will give me a clue as to how things are going to go with this particular occupant and the upcoming sale of the property. Sometimes the reaction is so bad that I recommend the seller to give them notice, get the property vacant, and then sell it. Jim's reaction was not a great one, but I felt he was workable. He said, "I can't believe Roy is doing this to me. I've lived here for twenty years!"

"Jim, I understand it is very frustrating; however, I do need to move forward. But I'll tell you what, let's have my partner Joy meet with you, and she can discuss the possibility of helping you relocate." He immediately calmed down. You have to remember that tenants can get very angry at real estate agents, almost like we are the bad guy or gal forcing them to have to move when in fact we are, of course, simply following instructions from the homeowner. It is important that the agent overcomes the tenants' fears and gains their trust as early on as possible. I made the appointment for Joy, and I will let her take it from here...

When I knocked on the door no one answered. I knocked again a little louder, still no one. I figured it was a no-show. Then as I started walking away, the front door slowly opened, and Jim stepped out. He apologized; he said he'd forgotten about the appointment and was taking a nap. Remember, the tenant is not the owner; they usually have zero motivation to help sell the property, and all too often, quite the opposite, some tenants have a lot of motivation to see the property *not* sell.

After looking at the house, I knew it needed more work than we'd anticipated. We sat at the kitchen table. Jim was nice enough, clearly not happy about moving, but he was not abrupt as some tenants can be. He said, "So, Dan said you can help me relocate?"

"Yes, absolutely, we do have a full-time agent on our team who works with all our buyers; she also works with tenant relocation, but," I said, "do not depend solely on that. I would recommend you start looking around on your own too." He said he had been doing so but that prices were too high, and he could not afford it. I told him we would do the best we could for him, and then I proceeded to talk about the selling process where it pertained to him.

I told him Roy agreed to not have agents come by just at any odd time, that they had to make an appointment, and that if he would make himself available on the weekends, then I could have agents come during a certain window of time, making the process as easy on him as possible (that often works out for everyone because we are still being able to take advantage of prime weekend showing hours). The only thing I asked is that he keep the place reasonably clean. Jim nodded his head in agreement.

The first weekend we had three agents who wanted to show their buyers the property on Saturday. I called Jim, left a message, but there was no reply; this went on for two days. I had to call Roy again and let him know; he was getting very upset with Jim. A few days later he called me back. "Okay, Joy, try him again; I told him if he cooperates I'll pay him fifteen hundred dollars for some of his moving expenses. I can't believe that with the cheap rent I was giving him all those years now I have to pay him to cooperate! I'm so upset!" I explained to Roy that this was somewhat common behavior and to try not to take it personally, but that I did understand that it could be frustrating, even kind of hurtful when you've been more than fair to someone, and he or she acts in this manner. I contacted Jim; he agreed to let the agents in. We had an offer that first weekend. Roy was elated because he had found an unbelievably great deal on another rental in his area with the agent I'd referred him to.

About a week into escrow, we needed to get back into the property for inspections. Jim was again unresponsive, missing in action. I generally try to get hold of tenants three times before I go back to the owner. After the third try, I had to call Roy. A few days later, I got the call. "Joy, I can't believe this unappreciative so and so said he ain't moving. I'll have to evict him; that could take months and a lot of money. I can't lose this property I'm buying out here; it's just too good of deal." I replied "Okay, well, first off, Roy, call an attorney who handles evictions, and while you are doing that, let me talk to Jim again."

It took a couple of days, but I finally got hold of him. I told him, "Jim, I would like to speak with you in person. I have some ideas that may help you." He reluctantly agreed, and we set up an appointment. Remember, although it certainly sounds like it, Jim was not a bad guy; he must have been terrified. Twenty years in the same place is a long time, and the cheap rent he was paying…he must have thought he would be paying that his entire life. I also think Jim was getting some bad advice from people.

When we met, the first thing he did was apologize and tell me that he really was not like this. He went on to say that all the properties we'd found for him as well as the homes he'd found on his own were all way too expensive. I asked him, "Jim, have you thought about buying your own place?"

He laughed. "I can't even afford to pay rent. How in the world can I buy?" He then went on to say, "I should have bought a place when I got out of the service twenty years ago."

"You're a veteran, Jim?" I excitedly asked.

"Yes," he responded.

"Well, first, thank you for you service, and second, you might qualify for a VA loan; you might not even need any money down."

He perked up a little but then kind of waved his hands and said, "Ah, doesn't' matter, Joy. I cant' afford the payments."

I replied, "How do you know that? Have you ever spoken to a lender?"

"Well, no," Jim said. "But I just know I can't."

I said, "Well, let's at least try; how's that?" I asked.

He agreed. I had my lender call him and after checking his credit and finances, the lender told me he had very little debt and good credit and that he couldn't believe he was renting. Often when a tenant has extremely low rent, the motivation to buy is gone; Jim was a perfect example.

We still had a problem though. The loan Jim could get would not come anywhere close to being able to buy anything in this area. I told him that, but I also told him about an area close to thirty miles east of here that was affordable for him. He said he knew that area and was actually okay with it. I asked him if it would be a problem traveling back and forth to work. He said, "No, I mostly work out of my house. I typically only go in one day a week for meetings." Jim found a place to buy in just a few weeks, and we were able to close escrow at the same time with Roy's home and his purchase.

This could have gone the other way. Roy might have had to spend thousands on an eviction and would have also lost out on a great deal on his purchase. It is *very* important that the real estate agent you hire to sell your rental understands how to deal with tenants. Diplomacy, patience, and yes, sometimes firmness is the combination you want to look for. The agent *must* ask questions, and he or she also must gain the trust of not only you the homeowner but also of your tenant.

Now you may be in a position where your rental property is vacant, so you do not have to deal with tenant issues. Although it is true that you will not have tenant challenges, a string of other issues surface where it pertains to unoccupied properties. Make sure when you are interviewing agents that they know how to handle tenants properly *and* also know how to give you valuable guidance when it comes to avoiding or at least limiting problems that can occur with vacant properties.

My Listing Expired with My Previous Agent

"I had my home on the market for months, and nothing!" I hear this quite often. True, expired listings can be more common in slow markets, but they do happen in strong markets too.

An expired listing can be extremely hard on the homeowner not to mention frustrating, especially when it seems that other homes are moving. They feel a sense of failure, like there is something wrong with their particular home or in many cases that there is something wrong with their agent, which is sometimes (but not always) the case. Many different reasons can lead to a home being on the market for months at a time and going unsold.

Most people think a house does not sell because of pricing and, to be honest, yes, that is certainly one of the more common reasons, but rest assured, it is not the only one. As I start preparing for expired appointments, I start eliminating reasons the home did not sell, one at a time, and eventually what is usually left are a few solid facts that speak loud and clear as to what happened. If we are able to convey these facts properly to the discouraged homeowners and they agree, the odds of the property selling become dramatically higher.

I have seen some absolutely stunning homes on the market that everyone thought would sell right away: the homeowner, the agent, the neighbors, everyone, but for whatever reason it did not. I would have to write another book just about why homes do not sell. It can go in a number of different directions: location, pricing, repair issues, city or neighborhood problems, traffic, and so on. Perhaps the agent left something very important out of the marketing, like the city! Yes, this can happen. The agent may not have done a good job at describing the property. Perhaps they do not know *that* particular market and certain catch phrases that are "in." Yes, I have seen plenty of expired listings where it was obviously the agents' lack of knowledge that most likely caused the home not to sell, but I have seen plenty other cases where in fact other factors, *not* the agent, were the problem. If that problem is identified, then it can be dealt with, and the property should subsequently sell.

If you had a home on the market that did not sell and you are reading this, I am very sorry and know the discouragement involved here. I also know the hassle you had to go through showing the home and keeping it clean only to be disappointed when no reasonable offer or in some cases simply no offers at all were made. Sometimes not even any showings, zero interest. I also know, only so well, that if you had a listing that expired, then you were probably deluged by real estate agents, calling, mailing, knocking on your door, sky writing their name above your house, whatever it takes to get you to talk with them. I know it can be very irritating. Personally, I rarely call or visit an expired listing unless I am asked to. What I will do is maybe have my assistant send a postcard in the mail, but that is usually the extent of it.

I do not fault the other agents for trying to get your business, and some may be very good agents whom you should consider interviewing, but as for myself, if an expired-listing client contacts me, then fine, I would love to have Joy or one of our team members meet with them. There is one thing that has always fascinated me about this same subject: if agents call on you *after* your listing has expired and say they have a buyer who wants to buy your home, then why the heck didn't they just show your home when it was on the market? Perhaps the agents truly don't have a buyer interested and it is just a ploy to get in the door? Maybe…if so, that is a blatant untruth being told to you, and I doubt anyone would want to work with such agents. If, however, for whatever reason, one really does have a buyer interested, then by all means entertain that; perhaps you do not even have to put the property back on the market. That might be an ideal situation for you.

Whatever the case, again, if your listing expired, it might have been the agent's fault, or perhaps, it was not. Until you have a professional experienced agent use certain formulas and tactics to find out what prevented it from selling, you will most likely go back on the market only to face more months of disappointment.

My suggestion? Wherever you are in the country, if your home did not sell, use the methods spelled out in this book to find new agent(s) to interview; they probably will already know, but if not, do tell them that you are a recently expired listing. Yes, you will be starting the process all over again, but I am confident if the agent hiring process is done correctly, you will end up on the winning side this time!

Expired-Listing Scenario
This is a case where our office was approached by a couple who had their listing expire with the previous agent. Their home had been on the market for well over four months with nothing, no offer, not even any showings; they were both very discouraged.

I did my research to prepare Joy for the appointment, and as it goes with many expired listings, proper preparation can be very time consuming. I have to investigate in a sense and, again, use the process of elimination to deduce why this home did not sell. I will say that often on expired listings, the reason is quite clear—a hugely inflated price or an absolutely horrible location, for example; it is quite obvious what happened, but this one was not such a case.

Yes, the house I admit was a little overpriced but not in an exaggerated way. I reviewed and analyzed, reviewed and analyzed, over and over again. I could not get it. This house may not have sold, but it certainly should have at least had a decent amount of showings on it. This was certainly not the first time I'd been stumped by an expired listing during the preparation process. Until Joy actually goes out there and sees what we are dealing with, we really don't know all the facts, enough anyway to come to a legitimate conclusion as to why it did not sell. Joy went out to the property, and I will let her take it from here...

I arrived at the appointment about an hour early. I typically do that to give myself time to really see the house from the outside in detail. In this case, there was nothing major—good or bad—that was coming out at me. I mean it did not look like a model home nor was it backed up to a supermarket, freeway, or what have you, and it was certainly not dilapidated. I did, however, notice a boat by the side of the house. "Hmm," I thought, "I don't remember seeing anything about boat or RV parking in the original listing." I double-checked right there and then, and nope, no mention of that type of parking. I proceeded to drive by some of the other homes that had sold in the area.

When the appointed time came, I went to the door. Susie answered, and I could see a gentleman I assumed to be Rob sitting in the living room watching the game. He was anything but enthused at my presence. Understand that expired listings have real estate agents practically crawling down the chimney. Susie apologized, and said "Rob, this is the one I talked to you about. I called them; they didn't call me." Rob shrugged his shoulder like he really didn't care, muted the volume, and slowly got up.

I then proceeded to do what I almost always do: I check out the house first. They both took me on a tour. It was a nicely sized home about twenty-five hundred square feet, average yard except for the boat/RV parking. As we made our way through the house, they pointed out what looked like a loft or bonus room upstairs; funny, I didn't remember seeing that in the listing either. I casually glanced at the old listing as we were walking through, and, well yes, the previous agent *kind of* mentioned it; he said there was a loft, and that was the extent of it. When they took me up there, it was anything but a "loft"; this was a full-fledged bonus game room with a pool table, wet bar, dart board, and the works. Rob was especially proud of it as he should be; it was beautiful. We left the bonus room and then proceeded to see the rest of the house.

It was average, nothing really special. The last place they took me to was the garage; they pointed out that it was oversized. It could fit two cars and then some. They converted that extra room into a very elaborate workshop for Rob. He was an avid woodworker. Again, I thought, "Was that in there?" In the original listing, I mean. I checked and yes, indeed it was, but all it referenced was an oversized two-car garage, nothing about the workshop. When I sat down with Rob and Susie, I did not go into my usual presentation; rather, I went straight for the facts. I told them I knew with quite a bit of certainty why their home did not sell. They said, "We know, we know, we've heard it a million times; the price is too high, right?"

"Nope, guys, I don't think that is it; yes, I think you are a little high, but again, I highly doubt that was the reason your home did not sell."

Now keep in mind that all they have been hearing from agents is "I have a buyer for your home," "Your price is too high," "I can sell your home fast," "List with me, and reduce the price, and we can sell!" so on and so on. But when I showed them the old agent's listing, they both kind of nodded their heads. Evidently no one else had done their homework. Rob and Susie had *no* idea those amenities were not being used appropriately or even accurately for that matter.

I could tell that both of them started to lighten up a little; I was not telling them the same things they had heard numerous times before. They said, "Joy, could that really make that much of a difference? I mean, the workshop, the bonus room, and the boat/RV parking?"

I told them, "Actually, no. I do not think any one of those alone made the difference in why your home did not sell but…all three of them together? Yes, I believe so. The buyer who wants this home is going to be a buyer with certain needs, a person or persons who enjoy the outdoors, a hobbyist, and someone who likes to entertain, often the three go hand in hand."

Rob had my full attention now and shut off the game; before he had just muted it. "Rob?" I said, "Will you leave the pool table?"

He thought for a moment. "I will, yes, but I want you to know that is no ordinary pool table; it's a completely refurbished antique."

I thought, "Why in the world would that other agent not have even asked about the pool table?" I continued, "You know what? Leave the price where it's at. Let's reduce in thirty days if we get no activity, but I'm going to have Dan do a write-up on this home and set up a professional photo shoot, and make sure *all* your amenities are photographed."

Now you may be thinking I am going to say we immediately received an over-full-price offer, and every one lived happily ever after. But the truth is, we did not get an offer. However, what we did get was *activity*. Agents were showing the property, and there was a bit of a "buzz" happening about Rob and Susie's home. Three weeks went by, and still no offer, but again sufficient activity. Rob called me and said that he and Susie were actually now getting excited about moving; before they thought it would never happen and so had become complacent about the whole matter. He told me they'd both agreed to just reduce the price now instead of waiting until the month was up. I processed the change in price, and about two weeks later, we finally got an offer—the first offer Rob and Susie had seen on their home for going on five months! Four months with their prior agent and about one month with us. There was some back and forth, but everyone finally agreed; the offer was not full price, but it was awfully close. Escrow closed, and Rob and Susie could not have been happier; they were very pleased. They'd never thought they would see this day happen.

The right buyers who were out there all along never even knew this home existed. Well, I take that back; they knew it existed, but they had no idea it had an RV/boat parking, a huge bonus room with an antique oak pool table and wet bar, and a workshop in the garage to boot! Not all expired listings are like this, but rest assured, many are, and the ones that are not…well, there's a reason they did not sell either. There is always a reason. Don't allow an expired listing to discourage you; find a competent agent with experience, skills, and instinct, not to mention good old-fashioned common sense, and you have a winning ticket.

For Sale by Owners: An Agent Magnet
I found in speaking with FSBOs (pronounced as "fizbos") over the years that many simply do not want to work with an agent, so I rarely even try to

convince them. I know for a fact that there are probably dozens of agents who have already tried to do so. I simply respect their choice to go at it alone and then let it go at that.

The only thing I want to offer a FSBO is a quick system to put together should there be *any* possibility of them deciding for whatever reason to list their home with a broker. A FSBO is in a *very* unique position that other homeowners are not. That position is a wonderful opportunity to add or eliminate agents from the interview lineup, again only if that FSBO thinks there is even an inkling of a possibility that he or she may take that route in the future.

If you are a FSBO, follow the below system; it's easy, not time consuming, and will pay huge dividends should you ever decide to list your home with a broker. The first thing you will need is a box; it could be any box but something like those boxes you find at any office supply store that holds files work best. Here is what I want you to do:

Phone Calls from Agents
If you answer the call, respond to the agent like this: "I'm sorry I am not interested in listing my home with a broker at this time, but just out of curiosity, if I was, can you give me three good reasons why I should list my home with you?"

Ask the question nicely and in a pleasant manner, but be serious about it. Make it very clear that you do not want an interview, that you do not want them dropping by the house, rather that you would like to know right now those three reasons. What this will do is help you separate the experienced agents from the not-so-experienced ones. The seasoned agent will have an immediate response; there will be no lag time or pause; reason one, reason two, reason three, boom...done! Does it matter what those reasons are? No, I really don't think so; just the mere fact that they had a response and did not have to think about it is, in my opinion, sufficient enough. They have no doubt been asked this question many times throughout the years and know how to answer it.

The inexperienced or low-producing agent? Highly unlikely they will have a stock answer, more likely they will fumble over their words while their mind is thinking of things to say.

Kindly thank the agent who gave you the professional response and ask to be mailed his or her card. The other agents? Just politely ask their name, thank them, and end the conversation. Write the inexperienced agents' names down and put next to them the word "No"; put that in the box. When you receive the card from the professional agent, if it came with any marketing material, take a quick look at it. If it looks professional, put it and the card in the box. If not, note on the back of the card "Unprofessional Material," throw away the marketing material, but keep the card. Why put the agents' names who did not pass the tests in the box? You will forget about him or her, and if the time comes that you do decide to hire someone, you want to know who *not* to call!

If you choose to, you can even make some quick notes on the agent, perhaps his or her response to your question, or even the mannerisms. That's it; you're done, no need to have any more communication with the agent *unless* you decide to start interviewing agents. Then you simply go to the box and pull out the relevant information.

Phone Messages from Agents

This is an easy one. If the agent left you with what sounded like a very professional and well-thought-out message, then jot the name and phone number down, and put that in the file box. No need to call them back; as a matter of fact, that may be a mistake. If you call an agent back, there is strong possibility they may start aggressively pursuing you. If the message was rather unprofessional, write the agent's name on a piece of paper with the word "No" next to it, and drop it in the box.

Visits from Agents

If agents come to your door, I would not recommend inviting them in unless of course you are having an open house. Tell them that you are not interested in their services but if you were, what three reasons could they give you as to why they were the best for the job. If they pass, take their cards, and place them in the file box. If on the other hand you were not impressed, thank them, accept their cards anyway, and put these also in the box, that's right, with the word "No" on them.

Direct Mail from Agents

A professional package? Save it, but again, do not call the agents to ask them to give you the three reasons. If you call them, they will think you are very serious about hiring an agent and will probably pursue you. Simply put the package in the box. A weak package? Same thing as before. Throw it away, but keep the card and write the word "No" on the back.

E-mail

If you had your e-mail address on any of your FSBO marketing pieces and you receive e-mails from agents, respond to them. Tell them you are not interested in their services, but if you were, to please tell you three reasons they were the right agents for the job. If you get a fast reply and it is professional, you have a contender for the job; print that out, and put it in the box. If, on the other hand, they take a day or two to get back to you, no matter what they say in that e-mail, it's a big fat "No." The unprofessional replies…same thing: print it, put "No" on it, and throw it in the box.

You now own a very valuable asset that other homeowners do not have, and it took you very little effort—that is, the names and numbers of real estate agents who impressed you as well as the ones who did not. Should you decide to list your home, go through the box, find all the positive notes you wrote, and check out their websites. If that looks good, talk to them directly on the phone; if you're impressed, they're in the lineup.

I hope my simple and easy system of adding and weeding out potential agents pays you big dividends should you ever decide to hire a broker. If you end up choosing not to, I sincerely wish you the best in that sale!

Senior Relocation

One of the largest investments people will own can end up being their home. I've seen this time and time again. What started as a sincere desire to enjoy perks of property ownership like tax benefits, pride of ownership, and so forth became in many cases a financial boom. Think about it: at one time a beautiful piece of property, for example, may have cost the new, young buyers a whopping $75,000. Well, it was certainly "whopping" at that time! I always get a kick out of the expressions I see on young buyers' faces when I tell them what I paid for my first home. What they don't understand is that the conditions were much different then. Income, of course, was in most cases much, much less than now, and the interest rates may have been through the roof.

The bottom line is that there is almost always a risk when buying anything. Just because the original price of a home by today's standards is minimal, at the time it could very well have been a big financial jump. That said, let's say this person who paid $75,000 for a home did not know that the geographical area would be unbelievably in demand due to a certain type of commerce or industry that would be subsequently created in that area. What was an average-priced home in an average neighborhood would be now anything but average. Some areas were not so fortunate as to have a commercial boom, but still, just normal appreciation alone may have caused the property to increase substantially in value.

So now, thirty or forty-plus years later, senior citizenship and a possible relocation have approached. What I have very often seen over the years is that many of these homeowners cannot afford the upkeep for their property, let alone the thought of even buying another home in their own area. Perhaps most of their retirement is indeed tied up in the property, and they have very limited income from any other source. Sure glad they bought that house all those years ago! This means staying in the area might not be realistic. Their real estate agent can help them determine a good relocation area for them and refer them to like-minded agents in areas the respective clients would like to move to. Helping a senior relocate simply comes with the territory in working with this kind of real estate sale.

Quite often, these seniors are widows or widowers; many have a family member or a very close friend helping out with the process, but some do not. Some, for whatever reason, are completely alone, and with that aloneness can come vulnerability; predators know this. I am not saying this to frighten anyone but rather to simply alert you to be aware of your surroundings when it comes to being approached by anyone with regard to finance or, in the context of this book, the sale of real estate. Just because people have complete capacity to make a decision does not mean that they cannot embrace the aid of a trusted person or entity. This is not just referring to seniors but really anyone. It's just good sense to knock ideas off people you trust. The best scenario, of course, is having people you trust along with some sort of legal representation.

Joy and I love working with seniors. It truly is one of the more rewarding aspects of our job. Think about it: this person, or persons, has contributed to society in various different ways and has now come to what should be an extremely rewarding, enjoyable, and yes, even introspective, period of one's life. If you are a senior thinking of selling and relocating, make sure you put your investment and future in the hands of the right real estate agent.

Where it pertains to the sale of a property owned by a senior, there are certain things I feel a need to express, and one of them is elder abuse. Seniors are the jewels of our society; it is my line of thinking that they are to be honored, respected, and yes, in some cases, protected. Most seniors I have come across in my years of selling homes have full capacity to make decisions; the ones that do not or are questionable...I will simply not work with them unless they have some sort of legal representation or even a family member who has certain legal powers to take care of things for them. If you know a senior who is, or seems to be incapable of making decisions, or if you have reason to believe any senior is being taken advantage of, please contact the appropriate persons who handle situations such as these for guidance and ultimately protection.

Now let's say we have a situation that does involve a senior who is not able to make his or her own decision, but there is certainly no fear of abuse or them being taken advantage of in any way. This senior has family or perhaps friends who want very much to make sure he or she is well taken care of on many levels and have made sure they are legally protected in an appropriate manner.

Very often the ones we work with are the children, but sometimes they could be nieces, nephews, friends, and so forth. For the sake of easier reading, in this section we will simply refer to the persons taking care of the senior as the children. Their parents can no longer make certain decisions or sometimes any decisions at all on their own or for whatever reason cannot physically take care of themselves, and there is absolutely no choice than to relocate them.

This can be an extremely emotional and sometimes even traumatic event for all parties involved. The children have to uproot their parents often from the home they, meaning the children, themselves were raised in. There are councilors available to help you and your parents through this difficult transition, and I think it would be well worth the effort to engage in that. There are also councilors who should be able to give you the proper guidance on the best place for seniors to be relocated to, whether it be another family members' home, some type of senior living, and so forth.

With regard to the sale of the home, you had better have a real estate agent who understands one very important word: "empathy." Without that the entire family is going to feel as though their parents' home, often the place where they themselves were raised, is now nothing but a business transaction—very similar to what can happen in a probate sale but with a different dynamic: that parent is still living; this could make things all the more challenging, emotionally and otherwise.

Yes, it is a business transaction; you definitely want as much out of that property as possible. Generally, the money from the sale is going toward the care of the senior. But a business transaction can also have an element of warmth to it. If only more agents understood how their actions, their tone of voice, and their presence can make a difference to an entire family, I think more agents would take this type of sale much more seriously. I would like to add one more comment regarding senior sales; I feel it is important for any home seller to have tax, financial, and legal advice, this *for sure* includes the senior. Often the money in their home is a large part of their retirement, having appropriate persons giving sound recommendations is highly recommended.

Senior-Relocation Scenario #1
I was asked by a mutual acquaintance to contact Howard directly because he was ready to sell his home, and he and his wife, Gladys, had plans for a very simple retirement in a senior community. The property they currently lived in was two thousand square feet on a pretty-good-sized lot. Howard

and Gladys were just barely seniors; they were still relatively young and healthy but felt that upkeep was just too much for them, especially as they saw themselves getting older, not to mention their home had two stories, and both felt it prudent to get into a single level instead. Neither of them had ever sold a home before; they bought this property when they were in their twenties.

When I called, Howard answered the phone; I knew just by the way he said hello that this was a very kind and gentle man. I introduced myself and told him that I was referred by so and so and that I would love to answer any questions he may have with regard to the sale of his property. He thanked me very much for calling but went on to tell me that they were in the process of negotiating a deal with someone who had come to their door last week. The hairs on my neck immediately went up, but I stayed calm and asked him if they had signed anything yet? "No, no, not yet, but my wife and I will be meeting with the person Wednesday evening to finalize everything." Now keep in mind Howard really did not know who I was; he did know that I was referred by a friend, but that was the extent of it. I asked him how much they were selling their home for to the buyer, and he told me; my fears were well founded. It was low, very low. I kept quiet and let him keep speaking. He said, "Dan, this buyer said it is an all-cash deal, and we don't have to pay agent fees and costs, so we think that is the direction we're heading."

Now, I found very early on in my career that it was crucial to stay calm in almost every situation, this most certainly being one of them. It was Friday, and they were not meeting this person until the following Wednesday, so I had a little time. I asked him if he would promise me they wouldn't sign anything until the allotted appointment, just to give me some time to do a little research. Howard said, "Nah, don't worry about doing research and stuff, Dan; I really think this is the way I'm going to go, but I sure do appreciate your call!" I found out later that Howard was from a very small town and moved out here to Southern California when he was a young man but that the small-town boy never left. Howard called things as they were but never in an angry or condescending manner. I spoke to him a little further on the phone, not wanting to end the conversation quite yet, and finally he said, "Okay, Dan, do your research, and call me back if you want, and I promise Gladys and I won't sign anything until Wednesday."

Now I already knew the price he told me that the buyer wanted to pay was well below value, but at the same time I had never seen the property; perhaps it was dilapidated. I drove by the very next day, and it was anything but. After some due diligence and already pretty much knowing their neighborhood, I knew that even with Howard and Gladys paying commission they were leaving about $80,000 on the table, basically handing over that amount of money to this individual.

I called him that very same day and told him; "Howard, I drove by your home; I did not come to the door because I did not want to intrude on your privacy, but you and your wife have a beautiful property, and I am extremely confident that I can get you an additional $80,000, and that is *after* you've paid commissions." But Howard, as gentle a man as he was, seemed to also be very stubborn. He said, "Thanks, Dan, but this buyer is coming over in a few days, and he said we did not have to pay any commission or fees." I stayed calm and reiterated my concerns but this time from a different angle. He was still not budging, and it began to dawn on me that they were both confused. Again, he and Gladys had moved into that home when they were in their twenties and had never sold a property before; they just did not understand how the sale of real estate worked, how commission and closing costs were paid from the sale of the property at the close of escrow and certainly not out of their own pocket.

So I finally said firmly but respectfully, "Howard, I can sell this home for you and Gladys, perhaps also to a cash buyer, and when escrow closes, you will be getting a check for $80,000 *more* than the check you will get if this buyer purchases your home and you do not have to come up with anything up front. There was a long and almost uncomfortable silence; at first I worried that perhaps he hung up on me but that would be completely out of character for him. He then repeated to me; "So, Dan, let me get this straight, you are saying that we will get $80,000 more if we sell our home with you than if we sell to this buyer who is coming over Wednesday? And we don't have to pay you anything out of our pocket?"

"*Yes!* That is exactly what I am saying!" I knew at that moment I was successful at helping Howard understand. It was not their fault they did not understand the process; rather it was mine for assuming that they did. I set up an appointment for Joy to meet with him and Gladys; she reexplained everything so there was no confusion, answered all their questions, and then proceeded to take care of the paperwork; about two months or so later, the house closed escrow, and Howard and Gladys received about $80,000 more than what they would have had they sold to the original buyer, who by the way approached Howard after the fact and was none too happy. The person who was trying to buy their home for well below market...was not happy, kind of ironic isn't it?

Now for some people, the extra money they received from the sale might not have made a huge difference in their lifestyle, but for Howard and Gladys? Well, it meant they could take a nice long vacation every year for the rest of their life.

I want to add one last element to this story. Because Howard and Gladys hired us, they had representation. We were their agents, and good thing, mold was discovered in their home. It was discovered early enough to where we were able to disclose it to the buyer, remediate the problem, and move forward to close. Had that not been discovered and Howard and Gladys had sold to the other person, they could have ended up not only losing about $80,000 from the sale but they may also have ended up in court losing much more of their nest-egg profits, fighting the buyer over mold. But all's well that end's well, and in the process I learned a very valuable lesson; not everyone understands how a real estate agent gets paid. I took that for granted. Howard was not stubborn. No, not at all, he and Gladys simply did not understand.

Senior-Relocation Scenario #2

In this particular situation, it was my partner Joy who was mostly involved with our client Edward, the potential sale of his home, and his relocation. Edward called our office and said he wanted to list his home and asked if Joy could come over the weekend. I said, "Sure" and then proceeded to ask him some qualifying questions. "First, Edward, why are you selling?"

"I finally retired, Dan! Thirty-five years at the company, and last week was my final week."

"Well, congrats! Where are you moving to?"

"Moving to Wisconsin; my daughter, her husband, and their three children, well, my grandchildren, live there. I'm really looking forward to this."

"Great," I said. "Let's have Joy come out Saturday afternoon."

"Perfect! Anytime, Dan; I'm retired!"

Joy went out, met with him, and did what she always does on interviews, and that was to try to better "get inside the clients' heads," find out where they are so she can better lead them in the right direction. I will let Joy take it from here…

Having worked with lots and lots of retired and relocating seniors, Dan and I both know what can happen if a move is made too hastily. I proceeded to ask some questions. I really wanted to know more before we moved forward. I mean, don't get me wrong; I was happy to list his home and sell it for him. That is what we do for a living, but sometimes in senior situations, haste can be a problem, or it could go the other direction. The senior is taking too much time making a decision, and especially if there are health-related issues propelling the move, that could be bad. This, however, was certainly not the case. Edward was ready to go. He went on to tell me that because of the distance (remember we are in Southern California), he had not really seen his grandchildren in about ten years. "Well, Edward, where are you going to live when you move back?"

"Oh, I'm moving in with my daughter and her husband; they have a huge home and even have a separate bedroom and bathroom downstairs, which is where I will be living, they said I could pay them a little out of my pension every month, and that it would help, as my son-in-law has been out of work for sometime."

"Well, that sounds like a good setup. How old are your daughter and grandchildren?"

"Well," said Edward, "let me think about that for a second. I would say my daughter has to be in her fifties by now. Gosh! How time flies, Joy! And the grandchildren...well, there are three of them, goodness they must be in their early to mid teens."

I decided to get off the family subject. "Well, again, Edward, I am very excited for you, but my gosh, Wisconsin gets pretty darn cold, doesn't it!"

"Darlin', I grew up back East. I was shoveling snow before I even learned to walk! I'll be fine. Although I will admit I will miss golfing with my buddies, but family is what it is all about, right, Joy?"

"No doubt about that, Edward," I said.

Okay, now do you see some possible potential problems Edward is facing? He is a widower, still very spry and active but certainly getting up there in years. He wants to move back to Wisconsin where the temperature can reach below zero, and he is going to live in the same house with his daughter and his out-of-work son-in-law and their three teenage kids, none of whom he has seen in over ten years. Sure, Edward grew up with freezing temperatures, but that was well over fifty years ago. He was certainly capable of making his own decisions, no doubt about that, but at the same time, my experience had taught me a thing or two, and I just wanted to make sure he was moving forward with full knowledge of what he was getting into.

"Edward," I said, "have you thought about maybe going out there to visit for a bit first and making sure you like it?"

"I did actually think about that, and thank you for bringing it up, but I have gone out there over the years when the Mrs. was alive. We would stay for two weeks or so and have a great time with our little grandkids."

"Well, perhaps," I said, "since you are retired and have some extra time on your hands, you can go there and stay for a month or two just to make sure you like it before you decide to sell your home?"

"Oh, I'm sure I'll like it, but I guess I could do that. I mean, I don't know...I really want to get going on this; I've been looking forward to retirement for thirty-five years."

"Okay, no problem; we will move forward anyway you would like us to, but here's an idea: let's go ahead, and list the property for sale; we can do all the paperwork right now, but just hold off going on the open market. Dan can start getting some marketing things ready, and I can give you some advice on little things you can do to your home in the next month or so to prepare it for the market; these minor changes will help you get the best price possible."

"Hmm…well, I suppose a month or so is not going make that much of a difference. Fair enough, Joy; actually that makes sense. Let's do that then."

Dan did what I said he would; he started preparing some marketing campaigns and the like. Edward did not leave right away; he followed my advice and did some minor things to his home first. About six weeks later, he called me. His voice was not the energetic voice I'd heard at our meeting. "Hello, Joy, it's Edward; you met with me last month. I am the guy who was going to move to Wisconsin; do you remember me?"

I laughed. "Of course, I remember you Edward! How are you, and how was your trip?"

"Well, Joy, not too good."

"What happened?" I asked.

"Well, those grandkids of mine? Ugh! I mean, don't get me wrong, Joy; I love them, but my gosh, the way they talk and that music they always have blaring and their friends…oh, Joy, their friends were the worst part of it; they were *always* over at the house. It was miserable. Not to mention the cold…I'd completely forgotten how that could be, especially when you're stuck in a house with three teenagers! I was going to stay a month, but I only lasted ten days. I was thinking…instead of selling and moving, I think I might want to get one of those reverse mortgages on my property; then I will have enough money to do some traveling and play more golf. I thought I could also fly my family out once a year or so, and they can stay with me for a while; then I can spend some quality time with my grandkids without all their friends around. Joy, I know I signed a contract with you to sell my home, but I really don't think I want to move."

"Edward, it's fine; don't give it a second thought. I'm just glad you found out now and not later after you had already sold your home and moved back there."

"Yeah, me too, Joy; me too."

Now this event was quite some time ago. Since then I received a call from Edward's attorney; Edward had passed away but had told his attorney to make sure there was a provision in his trust that stated that if anything were to happen to him that the house be sold with Dan and Joy at our particular brokerage. I was very touched and was extremely happy that Edward enjoyed the rest of his days playing golf with his buddies and still was able to have nice memories with his family.

So what does all this mean in the scope of choosing an agent to sell a senior's home? Be darn discerning in choosing the right agents for the forthcoming interview especially if you have not sold a home in a while, if at all. Some agents are actually certified in working with seniors from a real estate perspective. I personally like agents who have certifications in different areas. That is not to say that another agent cannot do as good or an even better job of selling the home, but it does mean that this particular agent took the time, effort, and money to at least try to better understand a certain specialty in the real estate sales industry.

I think the need for the right agent is very appropriate for this type of sale. That agent needs to be vigilant in making sure you are well taken care of before and during the transaction. If you are a senior reading this, always get proper tax and legal advice from qualified professionals, and use the method outlined in this book to find the absolutely best agent. Enjoy your golden years; you earned it!

"Integrity without knowledge is weak and useless and knowledge without integrity is dangerous and dreadful."

—*Samuel Johsnon*

4

THE ACTUAL INTERVIEW

I want to give you just a very brief history about myself. Over twenty-five years ago, I started with the Blanding Team. I saw quite a bit of potential in the "team" concept. Remember, at this time, many agents, like me, were basically working on their own, a one-person outfit, even under the umbrella of a brokerage. I did *everything* related to the sale of a home, and this kept me from giving my all to certain aspects of the business. I jumped at the chance to work as a team.

At that time, we decided that in order to properly represent our clients, Dan should manage the team office and take care of all the many "behind the scenes" duties while I would work directly with our clients. This is why Dan felt it best for me to work on this chapter with him since it's about the face-to-face relationship with the client.

So, let's move forward. You have used some of Dan's methods to locate some quality agents; now let's make some appointments.

Setting Up the Interview Appointments

You have now chosen a few agents who have passed the tests set forth in this book; it is time to book the appointments. Try to schedule them about three days to a week out. Occasionally we have potential clients call and ask if we can come out in a few hours to talk about selling their home. As difficult as it is for us, because we really do want to have a meeting with this person, we must decline. For real estate agents to be productive, they must have guidelines and systems to follow; otherwise it's simply chaos.

Again, I feel about three days to a week out is appropriate; anything less and you are putting a burden on agents to prepare for your appointment too fast; they may miss something important that may directly affect you. Also remember, you are not contacting just any agent. You have narrowed down real professionals. Professionals always take interviews with homeowners very seriously and prepare well for them.

I would recommend doing all interviews in one day, allowing approximately two hours per agent. Allow a little time between appointments; it can be a bit awkward for agents to cross paths at your doorstep!

Let's use Saturday for the interview example, but it can be any day. In this case since your appointment is on Saturday, Tuesday or Wednesday would be the latest days you would want to contact agents with whom you have chosen to set up for the interviews. Although you could set the times for whatever works best for you, I have found that most home sellers generally use the following time lines: the first one about 10:00–10:30 a.m., the next one between 12:30 and 1:00 p.m., and the last between 3:30 and 4:00 p.m. If you have a fourth, I would schedule that for another day; if you have only two (which is okay)—you don't necessarily have to interview three agents—then just schedule those two for a time that works best for you. Perhaps you only have one agent to interview, as no one else impressed you; there is nothing wrong with that, as long as that agent passed some of the tests in the line-up process and you feel comfortable and confident. Then go ahead, and interview the person; hopefully, he or she'll be the only agent you have to!

So now your appointments are all scheduled; do you confirm them? I wouldn't. My philosophy is that an agent should confirm an appointment with you, not the other way around. In addition, I feel they should confirm it one day, preferably two, prior to give you enough time to respond or reschedule, if something you have going on personally demands that. In other words, in this example, you should receive a confirmation call, text, or e-mail sometime on Thursday or Friday at the very latest.

Okay, you did well picking the agents, great job! Not a lot of home-owners can or even know how to do this properly. All three confirmed within a proper period of time, so you are on; they will be prepared, but are you? There are some things you must consider prior to the interview. Let's address them.

Preparing for the Interview

Websites

If you have not already, check your interviewees' websites before the appointment. Get a feel for their history, their service, their specialties, and so on. Look for a professional website, but avoid getting too caught up in the bells, whistles, and inconsequential photos.

I must share one story about an agent's website. Some time ago, we had a potential client whose home was foreclosing; now we do happen to have that experience, and I explained that, but the person, although appreciative of our skills and knowledge, decided to use another agent and proceeded to tell me who. We'd been around for decades in this area of Southern California and had never even heard of this agent. So, I did what any good businessperson would do: check out the competition.

I found their website, and I'll be completely honest with you: I was quite impressed. They had made claims about their experience, reputation, and production that were in a word, *awesome*; they had really nice photos and self-adulations. Well, as a member of our local multiple listing service, I can check an agent's listing production. Answer? Yes, they were some-what productive agents; however, they were not even close to the *perceived* success level their website was indicating.

I *do not* think they misrepresented themselves, technically anyway. But they used certain words and phrases that, in my opinion, lifted them up from an average-plus agent to a top-producing seasoned agent. It was then that I saw firsthand the power of the exaggerated use of "bells, whistles, and wowing claims" and how important it was for home sellers to be at least aware of certain types of marketing. I personally prefer basic to-the-point websites, not just in the real estate industry but in most other industries as well. Look for mostly useful "nuts and bolts" as opposed to inconsequential "bells and whistles."

Checking References

Often real estate agents will have "reviews" on their websites, marketing pieces, and so on. The questions you must ask yourself are these: Are the reviews valid? Who wrote them? Was it the agent's mother? Was it the agent? Again, I do not want to come across as cynical—rather, realistic. This could happen, and you should be aware of it.

I personally take reviews with a grain of salt, not just in the real estate industry but in many facets of commerce. If I am buying something off the Internet, for instance, and I review that product, I do take note of the reviews, but should I completely and 100 percent trust them? Let's spin this around for a moment. What if you see a bad review for an agent? Does that mean the agent is bad? Maybe, but maybe not. Sometimes people can be vindictive for no real reason or maybe a "perceived" reason that is not the reality. That said, perhaps if you see a long trend of reviews good or bad, then you can begin to take them a bit more seriously. For the good reviews, I would be optimistically skeptical and the bad reviews…well, if you are seeing a trend of these type reviews and they are coming from different persons (sometimes one person is so upset they leave multiple negative reviews), then yes, I would seriously take that into consideration.

The best reviews in my opinion are of real estate agents who have proven to be successfully selling homes for a lengthy period of time and in all markets and who have clean records with the Department of Real Estate. That's impressive! In my opinion, professionals do not necessarily need reviews. I mean, it's nice, but I don't feel it's a necessity. Again, they have already proven themselves to be honest and reliable solely by the length of time in the business, regularity of transactions, and license status.

Know Your Questions Beforehand

We've provided a list of important, to-the-point questions for you to ask *after* the presentation. Some may apply; others perhaps not, but this will give you a working idea of what needs to be addressed before you make any kind of decision on who you will hire to sell your home. I would like to point out that there is a chance you may not have to ask any at all. Most efficient agents will likely have already addressed a lot of questions in their presentations; this is why I recommend asking them after the presentation.

Open Houses

Do you want open houses? If so, you should know that prior to the inter-view, so you can ask agents if they will indeed hold an open house for you, and if so, how often. But let's pause here for a moment. If you have decided that you want open houses, then you must ask yourself if you are completely sure. Let me expand on that.

I've been fortunate to have been in this industry during the formative years, between pre-, early-, and post-Internet. Pre-and early-Internet gen-erally meant paper advertisements of your home. Often there was a quick write-up in a local newspaper along with a photo; if you were lucky, it was color, but often it was black and white.

I think open houses in a way kind of picked up the slack for that lack of exposure. Potential buyers *did not* have the luxury of getting online and within minutes, if not seconds, narrowing down a group of homes in the exact neighborhoods they wanted, all with color photos and virtual tours. Rather these poor buyers had to gas up the car and start driving around, keeping an eye out for open house signs. We do not have the same chal-lenges today as we did then.

We have found that selling a home from an open house was not that common then and is not that common today either. Why? You must ask yourself why these buyers are driving around on the weekends looking at houses? In my opinion it's because, among other things, human nature; buy-ers will often drive by houses they can't afford. So, in general, the open house attendees may very well not actually be qualified or for that matter even interested in purchasing a home; these buyers are just kind of *lookin' around.*

You must also ask yourself a very important and obvious question. Why isn't this person with a real estate agent? I think a serious buyer would be. You do not want a wishy-washy person making an offer on your home. Perhaps real estate agents won't work with this buyer because the buyer cannot get a loan and consequently has no choice than to go at it alone. I cannot tell you how many buyers I've seen walk into an open house very interested in buying the property even to the point of literally wanting to write an offer right there and then on the kitchen table, only to find that this person had some serious credit issues or was maybe not even employed! There is, of course, the question of security. Are you comfortable having just anyone right off the street walk into your home? Agents sometimes can have multiple persons at one time in the house; there is no way they can watch everyone. This means people could go anywhere in your house they like without anyone watching them...something to think about.

So why do agents do open houses if, relatively speaking, they do not seem to be that fruitful? Aside from the hopefully obvious reason that the agent thinks it might sell your home, I believe there is another answer: real estate agents are in the business of meeting new people and making new contacts. What better way for agents than having potential clients come to them as opposed to knocking on doors or cold calling on the phone. Farmers especially love open houses for a very good reason: huge exposure.

Open houses were and still are a good source of business for the real estate agent. So now, after reading this, do you still want one? If so, I can pretty much guarantee you that every one of the agents you interview will agree. In general, I would agree; however, I will tell you my feelings about it first.

Let me be very clear: aside from potential security issues, open houses certainly will not hurt and *could* help. I just want you to be aware of a few things before making that decision. You want agents using their time, energy, and money on things that will directly help *you* get the right price for *your* home. Is an open house one of those things, or is it going to benefit the agent more than yourself? Again, just some food for thought.

Lockboxes (Also Known as Key Boxes)

I try not to push this issue. Some clients are simply leery about having a key to their home being accessible to multiple agents. That is a personal decision, and I respect it. Bottom line, a lockbox *will* help you sell your home and will be less taxing on you. Lockboxes, if appropriate, are an absolutely wonderful tool. I bring this up to potential clients, but I do not force the issue.

Internet Marketing Websites and Social Media

Much of Internet marketing is automatic. A listing gets submitted into the multiple listing service and then generally is *automatically* uploaded to various real estate websites. (Do ask agents if their particular MLS systems do this.) Don't let agents convince you that they are personally putting your listing on all websites; there is a high probability they may not be. It is often automatic, so ask questions. Now that said, what the agent *inputs* into the MLS is vital. They need to be able to convey an attractive yet accurate description of your home that will grab a buyer's attention to explore further.

Wording is not the only way to convey a description. The old saying "A picture is worth a thousand words" most certainly applies here. The purchase of a home is typically a very emotional one. Find out how this agent will take and present photos of your home. Personally, we typically hire a professional company to arrange a photo shoot and subsequently present those photos in a very appealing manner. This is what they do, and I trust their specialization. As an agent, I do not wear the hat of a photographer. I have found that most top producers follow the same line of thinking. There is nothing wrong with your agent doing photos on one's own, but I just think, in general, it's best to utilize the services of a professional company.

All this said, is there Internet marketing the agent can do independent of what the MLS may do? Yes, but aside from perhaps very unique situations, I personally would not put too much stock in that; understand that some of the real estate websites out there are in a word *massive*. Some of them simply dominate the market—REALTOR.com, for example. They have a huge amount of market share and goodwill, a very strong and powerful combination. I remember my first broker, over thirty years ago, told me; "Joy, do not argue with success; success breeds more success." I've thought of that often over the years, and that frame of thought has always proven to work well. As long as the business practices are fair and honest, I do not argue with success; rather, I follow it, and consequently my clients end up on the winning side.

Many agents will tell you about their own website and how your home will be advertised on it. Well, that's okay, I suppose, but I really think in the end, it makes the agent look good. But is it helping? I'm not saying that your home advertised on a particular agent's website is not going to help you, but I would say the likelihood is quite small.

This takes us back to "success"; look for agents who put their energies into tried-and-true methods that have proven successful year in and year out. It's just a better investment with a much higher probability of getting the return in the form of a fantastic price and great terms for your home. The proficient agent will expand on those tried-and-true methods to meet your own personal needs.

Now I do not in any way wish to put down or lessen the marketing tactics of other agents; listen to what they have to offer, but just try to urge them to zero in on what is most productive when it comes to marketing and selling *your* home. I just don't want to see you put too high of an expectation in things that will likely not help. Same goes with social media; there is definitely benefit in social media, and our team certainly utilizes it where and when appropriate, but just know where that benefit is geared toward. Is it mostly promoting you and the sale of your home or mostly promoting the agent? As I have stated before, I am simply giving you some things to think about.

Area History

This is really something that you must get comfortable with yourself. As Dan pointed out in chapter 2, there are various types of agents: the agent you have past experience with, the seasoned agent, the personal referral, the farmer, and so forth. If you have, for example, a seasoned agent with a great reputation, then personally, I would not get too hung up on exactly how many homes they've sold in your particular area. This type of agent gets a lot of referrals and repeat business, so geographically they could be in a wider area. Many agents have very successfully ventured off into other areas. That local down-the-street and around-the-corner "Ma 'n' Pa" type of real estate office is no longer relative in many cases. This is a very good thing for you as the homeowner; your choices for quality real estate agents have increased dramatically.

I will say, however, that there is a limit. I mean, I would think you would not want an agent whose office is a hundred or so miles away to help you sell your home. We have been asked many times to list a home that was very much farther than the norm. These clients insisted on using us because of our experience and reputation or perhaps we came highly referred. Whatever the case, we could have done it, but in the end, it would not have been fair to that homeowner. Having to book a flight to go see a client would *not* be in the client's best interests!

But let's get back to "area experience"; are there exceptions? Why yes, although I have not seen this often, there are certain areas with issues that are very unique to just that area. For instance, I know of some neighborhoods that have had major soil problems; using an agent who understands this challenge is crucial. Or perhaps this group of homes was involved in some sort of class action lawsuit; utilizing the services of the area specialist would be a very smart move.

How Many Homes Annually

Note that I refer to "annually." I prefer this. Ask how many homes the agent has listed and sold in the past twelve to twenty-four months. The reason is that an agent may have just happened to have had a great month or two prior or even a great year; the numbers will then be deceiving. A well-seasoned agent typically sells homes all year round, every year.

I will be honest with you: this question about "How many homes sold" will be a very uncomfortable question for agents if they are not what they originally represented themselves to be. There are many agents who try to give the impression that they are more proficient and skilled than they are, but in the final analysis, they simply are not, and if confronted with this question, they can show some discomfort, which will help answer your question right there and then with regard to sales production. You will probably pick up on that discomfort immediately, especially by their body language or the tone of their voice. However, if you were diligent in your efforts to pick agents to interview, then you may have already received the answer to this question about productivity and will consequently not need to bring it up at the actual interview. Also keep in mind, the answer to the question about productivity can be relative to your geographic area. I really do not think there is any kind of rule to this—that is, how many homes sold. In my experience if an agent is listing and selling two or more homes a month, that's good, less than that? Yeah, you should still be okay, but I do not think too much less. Again, the answer to this could differ depending on your geographic area or the current market conditions.

If it's more, great, but if it's too much, then what is that telling you? Perhaps if you list with this agent, you will never hear from him or her again. For huge producers, there is an army of assistants and often other agents who are helping them. This agent simply will not have the time to give you that much personal attention. Is that a bad thing? No, not at all, it's up to you, that could be an outstanding agent. If you're okay working directly with an assistant or another agent, then you should be fine; there is absolutely nothing wrong with that. There's a good chance that mega agents, by the mere fact that they are successful, are probably carefully watching over everything anyway, so you should still be very well represented; its' just that you're communicating with someone else in the day-to-day dealings and activities that go along with a real estate transaction. If you feel you need that particular agent who is personally going to be right there for you, then you may want to avoid the megaproducer. We are all different, and things that may be important to you as a home seller will not be as important to another.

How Long the Agent Has Been Actively in the Business
Some agents have been licensed for decades but perhaps were inactive for years and are now just beginning to start up again. So simply ask them if they have been *active* the whole time; it's a yes or no answer. This is an important factor.

How long should they have been in the business? In my opinion, to properly represent you as a seller, no less than ten years, but this is not a hard-and-fast rule, and again, it's just my feelings from years of observation. Remember, chances are, depending on your geographical area and market, the first five years give or take, that agent was probably working mostly with buyers. The buying end of a transaction is much different than the selling end. That means this agent with a current total of ten years in the industry really has only about five or so years' experience working with sellers, not a huge amount of time, but I think sufficient—as long as they've been doing a relatively regular amount of business.

Systems in Place
We, as most top agents, only work with systems. I would highly recommend you find out from your potential agent what kind of systems they have in place. You may ask, and rightfully so, systems for what? Here are just a few questions you should ask about this subject:

- What systems do you have to give us market updates?
- What happens if an agent wants to show my home?
- What happens *after* that agent shows my home?
- What happens when a buyer calls you off our sign or your marketing pieces?

- What systems do you have after we have accepted an offer?
- What systems do you have to communicate with us? (extremely important inquiry)

The questions can go on, but these I think are the most important. Systems are a necessity to a successful real estate transaction. Look at it this way: We are all familiar with fast food restaurants, I mean, one of the many huge chains out there. You know how they work; you order a certain food item, and immediately an almost perfect *system* goes into place from the time you verbalize your request to the time you receive your order. None of these franchises could exist without systems. Why would running a real estate office and representing sellers in the sale of their homes be any different? I can tell you right now: they are not. Systems are a necessity.

Yard Signs
A personal decision, likened to open houses but I think stronger. I would say that they are not *as* important as they were pre-Internet, but that said, they still hold a decent amount of value. Often a neighbor will know someone who has been wanting to buy in your particular area or perhaps your house will catch the eye of a passerby. Also, logistically it makes it easier for the agent and buyers to find your home after they have made an appointment to see it. In addition, psychologically it lets the buyer know that indeed you are serious about selling. All that said, if you choose not to have a sign for whatever reason, it's not the end of the world, but truly, it can help.

Communication
I saved this for the last purposely. It is absolutely imperative that your agent has good communication skills. This is the number-one complaint I have heard clients tell me as they talk about their prior agents. "I listed my home and never heard from my agent." Now I will say that they most likely did not mean that in the literal sense. I'm sure that agent did speak to them after they listed the property; the question is how often and why?

The "how often" is much more important than the "why." An outstanding agent will have a contact system in place.

Let's use our communication system as an example. In general, our home sellers get a phone call, text, or e-mail from us every Monday and Friday. The choice of phone, text, or e-mail is the clients', whatever they are comfortable with. Why Monday and Friday? Much of the activity in the real estate industry happens on the weekends. These are typically the days buyers and agents alike have aligned themselves to view properties, thus the Friday communication. We then contact those agents on Monday mornings to get valuable feedback, which we share with our clients: Were their clients interested? If not, why? What did they think about our pricing? I ask a lot of questions; good buyers' agents are experts at representing buyers, and I respect and admire their knowledge. Their input truly can help my clients get the best possible price for their home.

Are these the only days we contact our clients? No, not at all; if necessary, we contact them at other times. Although there are always exceptions, for the very large part, these are the days they can pretty much set their watch that they will get a communication from us. Then, depending on the particular situation, we will e-mail our clients typically in the middle of the week with a market update.

What does all this mean? It means that, in general, our clients get a contact from us about every other day. Regular systematic communication between agents and their clients is essential. Ask your interviewees what systems they have in place to communicate with you. It certainly does not need to mirror ours, but if they do not have a stock answer, you could have a problem.

Returning Calls, Texts, and E-Mails

How long should you wait for a return call, text, or e-mail from your real estate agent? This is a very important question to ask at your interview. Typically, the answer should be as soon as possible, but how do you define that term? Every agent is different, so I cannot speak for all of them. For me personally, and I think most top producers would probably agree, although there may be exceptions, for the most part, one to two hours is the maximum wait time, certainly sooner if possible. If it's very late in the evening and not urgent, then the following morning should be appropriate, but it must be one of the very first calls of the day.

What Can I Do to Make My Home More Marketable?
A professional will be able to advise you as to the things you should do and equally as important the things you should *not* do. Often a potential home seller "fixes" or makes replacements on the wrong things. This could end up being a very big mistake—that is, they may have spent much more time and money on something that really should have been left alone. Trust the experts to advise you on how to prepare your home for the market.

An experienced agent has a lot to offer, tricks of the trade, so to speak. For instance, removing family photos to help de-personalize the property should be something you would want to do. You don't want buyers to feel as though they are infringing on your personal space; in addition, you want them to envision photos of *themselves* or *their* family within the home. There are many things you probably have never even thought about. Another example would be decluttering the property, thereby making the home appear much more open and light and with more usable space. These are just a couple of examples; the list goes on. My point is again, trust the experts, and if you adhere to some of the advice in this book, that is exactly who you should be working with: experts.

More questions? Sure, but what I am giving you are what I feel are the most important, direct questions that should be put forth and answered. If you have other questions you feel you should ask, then by all means, do ask. This is your home and your interview. To be honest, I've had many clients who have asked no questions, *none*; I had to pretty much coach them for their own good. I tell them, "Here are some questions other sellers have asked me." And then I proceed from there.

I *really* want homeowners to get the answers that they deserve to have. Exceptions about asking questions? Yes, quite often clients have already been sold on us and are simply having me over to list the home—no presentation and no questions necessary. In this case, I will only bring up the most basic of questions and their appropriate answers and move forward as this seller clearly does not need nor want to have the "traditional" inter-view. If this is the case for you, then consider yourself very fortunate to have found someone you already trust to do the job and do it right. Just one little piece of advice: if this is a specialty sale—for instance, you are facing some sort of hardship, whether it be divorce, foreclosure, or so forth—then even though you love *and* trust this agent, please make sure he or she understands the inner workings of your particular needs. You will be better off in the long run with the proper experience.

Commission

I know it is generally on people's minds, as it should be. My goal here is to simply give you a few things to think about. We are going to be referring to a real estate commission percentage; this is based on the sale price of the home, a negotiable rate that is not fixed.

Ask Just One Question: Why?

I cannot emphasize this enough: always remember to ask questions with regard to commission and subsequent service.

Ask, Ask, Ask! And allow the agent to ask questions as well. The more clarity as to the "why" a certain rate is being charged the better the chance you and your agent will both be comfortable with the commission charges and most importantly, that your mutual decision will not affect the salability of your home.

Things can get very confusing for you in today's fast-moving world. Between, the Internet, radio, mailers, television, and so forth, it's hard to know what to believe with regard to commission. For example, you may have a brokerage quoting what sounds like extremely low rates or perhaps offering some of kind program that seems very confusing to you, and con-versely, another that is quoting what sounds like comparatively really high rates. What do you do? Again, I recommend asking the questions you have learned in this book and even your own personal questions, but I have to tell you, the real estate sales industry can be quite complex, so unless you are actually in the industry, it would almost be impossible to know everything to ask. So aside from the more basic questions, make it easy on yourself; ask just one question, and let the agents take it from there. You should know by the responses, just how legitimate or honest their answers are. Simply ask "Why?"—that is, "*Why* are they quoting that rate? How is that rate going to help me as the homeowner get a great price for my home and at the same time give me the best representation possible?"

Ask them *why* some brokerages are charging more, and conversely, *why* some are charging less. That agent is offering you service and asking you to pay a certain amount of money for that service. Don't you think you should know the whys and the what-fors? I do, as do most professionals.

As for myself, I will never make sellers feel bad for asking me these questions; rather, I strongly encourage it. How are they supposed to know about all this stuff? Now in many, many cases, our clients ask what we charge; we tell them, and they say, "Okay." There is not a need to embellish on the subject because the clients already know us. There is a trust level there; they are already sold on what and who we are and what we do and feel our rate is fair, especially in light of the fact that they probably already know about trending commission rates in the area.

To be honest, in my experience, many professionals, depending on the situation, are willing to at least discuss the commission with you and do their best to make sure you are indeed happy with the rate you are paying. Although it is the agent's and brokerage's final decision—that is, to reduce their particular normal rates or not—they should also know that sometimes being too rigid can backfire and perhaps cause unnecessary ill feelings. Every situation is different.

Know what you are getting for your money, and as importantly, find out if there is something you are not getting. The bottom line is that I cannot answer these questions for you—that is, what commission rate you should pay—but do consider some of the factors in this section when discussing the subject. Go with your gut and common sense, and I think you will be fine regarding commission.

Get Top Dollar, Close Escrow, and Never Have to Look Back

Being represented properly is a vitally important factor in a real estate transaction. Let's address an example of the term "safely represented" for a moment. Dan mentioned toward the beginning of this book that the absolute worst thing that can happen in a real estate transaction is problems that surface *after* the fact—in other words, after escrow has closed. This is in a word, a nightmare—financially and otherwise. If you do not want to see potentially tens of thousands of dollars of *your* equity fly out the door, then make darn sure that the brokerage you hire has systems in place that will best mitigate the odds of after-close challenges to occur. I cannot stress this point enough. Can an agent's brokerage quoting a commission much lower than others afford to have those systems in place? Ask them; this is an extremely important question.

Let's face it, obtaining top dollar is the main goal for any home seller. My advice again is to look at what is trending: Are homes that are offering lower rates selling as fast and for top dollar as much as homes that are offering higher rates? More importantly, are those homes closing escrow? Again, agents should be able to show commission trends and their subsequent results. Does this mean you have to pay what the trend seems to be in your area? Of course not; the commission is not fixed. Should you pay what seems to be the trend? Well, if it seems to be working in your area with positive results, then perhaps so, but that is a decision you must make and no one else.

Ask agents what they charge. If it sounds agreeable for the service they are offering and for their experience and knowledge and you are comfortable, then move forward. On the other hand, if you have reason to believe you can get the *same service and attention* for a lower commission rate, then simply ask agents if they would consider charging a different rate.

Professional agents will respond and should respond, well...professionally. If they and their brokerage feel they can reduce commission from the normal rate they charge, and it should not make that much of a difference to the end result and both you and agent are comfortable with it, then great! If, however, they tell you that too much of a discount could possibly cause more harm than good, then ask them why; let them explain, and then at least consider what they have to say before making a final decision, but do ask them to explain. You certainly deserve to know.

Trends and Why a Broker Might Quote a Certain Rate
I would recommend that you look at the trends in your area, about what most sellers are offering. Your interviewee should be able to show that to you. How much a real estate brokerage and the agent are going to end up really making on the sale of your property can go in many different directions depending on several factors. For instance:

- Broker-REALTOR® agreement on the commission split
- Broker office policies
- Broker overhead
- Licensing fees
- Broker liability insurance
- Employees
- On staff attorney
- Multiple listing service dues
- Agent overhead
- Price of your home
- Specialty sales (foreclosure, probate, divorce, etc.)
- Marketing and advertisement costs
- Office rental

The list can go on, but I really wanted to give you some feel for the many varied reasons why a real estate agent might quote a certain rate. There has always been a misconception, and one I completely understand, that an agent will net the same amount of the commission that is being charged. That is rarely the case.

For one, if there is another agent involved representing the buyer, which is often what happens if your home is listed in the multiple listing service, then, depending on your listing agreement, the commission you are paying might be split in half between the two real estate agents and again, there are quite a lot fees involved in the real estate industry that need to be paid prior to the agent realizing their net pay. This is actually a very good thing; you want agents to have a lot of appropriate overhead. That means they are taking their job seriously and spending money to make sure their clients are being taken well care of on many levels:

Services and Hidden Value in the Real Estate Agent
If you have seasoned agents, for instance, who have obvious experience and a great reputation and they are telling you that they recommend a certain commission amount and a newer agent or firm, perhaps one you are not familiar with, that has only sold a handful of homes tells you a much lower commission rate, then you must ask yourself, "Is it too good to be true? Am I really going to save a few thousand on commission and end up with the same results?"

I want to make it abundantly clear that in no way would I discourage you from hiring an agent who is charging less than others, but at the same time, I want you to think about some things. On the surface, it looks like both these agents are offering the same service, but are they, in fact, *offering the same service?* Also, is there some *hidden* value in the more experienced agent that you might not be taking into consideration? What do I mean by *hidden value?* Are there things that a more experienced and knowledgeable agent can or will do that perhaps another simply will not or more likely just *cannot* do?

Many of these hidden attributes of a great agent are subconscious, so much so that often even they, the agents, cannot really articulate what it is. It's a line of thinking that is just second nature to the professional. For example, seasoned agents, by the mere fact, of their time and sales in the industry may see something in your house that neither you nor the other agents can see. If there is something positive, they will bring that up to you and show you how they can really use that to draw in as many buyers as possible and thus get you a better price. On the other hand, if they see something negative, they will address that with you and advise, whether to replace, repair, or show you that what seems like a negative is actually not and can work even better to your benefit. A professional should recognize that.

Experienced agents also know you might be able to get more for your home than what everyone else, including you, the homeowner, thought. What that is can often not even be anything physical; it may rather be something hard to define or put your finger on. Again, sometimes even for the agents, they kind of *just know*. Understand that a very skilled agent has an instinct or sixth sense for certain things pertaining to value and so forth.

I will never forget a home inspector I had worked with years ago. He had been around a long time, and I met him at a house we had sold so I could see firsthand what his findings were. It was an older home, and I was observing the way he was comfortably going through it, room to room, as if he himself owned and lived in the property. I was very impressed at how easy he was making it look, but at the same time how detailed he was.

I told him I was amazed at how he knew exactly where to look and what to look for in a home that he had never even been to before. He said, "Joy, you are no different." I really didn't understand what he was getting at, but he articulated further. "Joy, you make it look very easy; that is how you go about selling a home, but it is not easy. You just think it is because it has become second nature to you. I am the same way with my inspections." He was right. I had taken my expertise and that sixth sense that I'd developed over the years for granted.

This same line of thinking goes beyond staging and pricing a home and well into any real estate transaction. For example, let's say during the negotiation phase of your transaction, your very competent agent uses a certain tone of voice with the buyer's agent that basically says, "Countering us with a lower offer from our already very fair counter would not be a good idea." Suddenly with one inflection in your agent's voice, you've saved thousands of dollars—once again, *confidence* at work!

Perhaps it's later in the escrow and a buyer feels the need to ask for a $10,000 reduction in price due to some things discovered during inspection. Even though it was an "as is" sale, the buyer or the buyer's agents or maybe even one of those outside influences addressed earlier in the book, felt a need to try to squeeze some money out of you, the seller, especially now that everything is near to closing, and you have already purchased another home.

Let me pause here for one moment. Do not think for an instant that these types of things do not happen; they most certainly do and on a much more regular basis than you might imagine. Having an agent who can recognize and knows how to deal with these types of deceptive negotiation tactics is very powerful, resulting in more money in your pocket.

Back to the scenario: So, now what? The buyer's making noise to cancel if the 10K reduction is not accepted; you've got a smoking deal on the house you are purchasing, and there is no way you are bailing out of it, so you tell your agent, "Fine, give them the money; let's get this over with." But this is not your agent's first rodeo, so to speak. Perhaps there are times to give in to certain things, but this, the agent knows, is certainly not one of them.

Your agent's experience in this type of situation is very strong; he or she knows just from the way the buyer's agent presented this "new deal" that it is most probably bogus or at the least an exaggerated request and that it is highly unlikely the buyer is going to cancel because of it. Your agent also knows that those things on the inspection they are complaining about are probably minor and has an army of contractors willing to make the inspection or perhaps speak directly with the initial inspector. The result? With your permission the agent is going to do a little extra negotiating on your behalf. It could go something like this:

Your agent to buyer's agent: "That is just not going to happen—the ten-thousand-dollar reduction in price, I mean, but what we will do out of goodwill and to make sure everyone is happy is go ahead and give your buyer a two-thousand-dollar credit to appease some of the concerns on inspection."

The buyer's agent is no dummy; he or she can read between the lines and would know just by the demeanor of your agent as well as by his or her calm yet very firm tone that not pushing the money issue would be a wise move. "Okay, done," stammers the buyer's agent.

Now what just happened? Your proficient agent took complete control; he or she saw what was happening but still did not want to take any chance of you losing your new purchase yet did not want to see you taken advantage of either. Result? You saved $8,000 you were willing to give up. Again, make no mistake; this kind of thing happens in the real estate industry, and all too frequently, and an inexperienced agent may have no clue how to deal with it. This is one of many examples of how agents with longevity in the business and an abundance of experience can be worth their weight in gold. This is exactly what I mean by *hidden value*.

Now you know some basic questions to ask, and your appointments are all set up. It's Saturday morning, and you are ready to go, but wait, your agent is late. Really?

Is the Agent on Time?

My philosophy is that you can allow a little wiggle room on the time, but certainly not more than a few minutes—ten to fifteen minutes tops. Exceptions? Sure. Sometimes agents will be coming from another interview that simply went longer than normal, or perhaps they were servicing one of their existing clients with a very urgent situation, or perhaps they hit unexpected traffic. Although agents should pace themselves so they have plenty of time between appointments, these things do happen from time to time. Whatever the case, if I were in this situation and running a few minutes late, you should expect a call from me apologizing and letting you know that I'm a little behind.

Don't punish agents too harshly if this happens, but if they arrive late without making the call, strike one in my opinion. If they make that call but tell you they will be later than thirty minutes from the original appointment time, I would suggest you tell them that you need to cancel. Remember, you are on a relatively tight schedule; you have other agents coming, or perhaps you just have personal business to attend to. Whatever the case, anything past thirty minutes, I think for the most part, is unacceptable.

To be honest with you, I usually try to be an hour or so early! No, I do not go to the door until the appointed time, but I am there very early. Why? Aside from not wanting to take any chances being late, I want to see what my potential client's house looks like on the outside, both good and bad. Now typically, I'm already familiar with the house and the neighborhood, but still, I want to take a closer and keener look at certain things. Sometimes I will even go by the home days or, if applicable, even weeks before the appointed time to get an overall feeling about the property. But now, right before the appointment, I need things fresh in my mind. I need details, for instance, "Does it back up to a busy street or commercial property?" "Are there electric wires running through the backyard?" "After taking a closer look, does there seem to be a lot of deferred maintenance?" "Are there positives that I was not aware of? Does it have a beautiful circular driveway with obvious professional landscaping giving this home *major* curb appeal? Is it located on a cul-de-sac perhaps? How does the house sit on the lot?" I need to assess as much information as possible to accurately put a value on the property.

If I have not already, I will generally drive by other homes during the hour or so before my appointment that have sold or are currently on the market, homes that are best comparable to that of my client's. "Do they have the same negatives or positives that I just viewed outside my potential client's home? How does that affect value, either up or down?" These are very important questions.

Okay, let's assume everyone was on time. On to the interview, right? Wrong, in my opinion. Agents have their own way of conducting themselves at interviews, and I respect that, but how can one jump into the interview and talk about your home, it's value, and so on without seeing the property first?

Viewing the Property

Of course, agents are going to, along with the presentation, give you an estimation of value. Again, how can they do that without viewing your home and without you pointing certain things out, negatives and positives alike? Agents can't, so they should want to "take a tour" of your home before anything. How long should that take? Depending on the size of the house, I would say an average for me would be about twenty to thirty minutes, and that is for an average-sized home. Remember, this is *not* an all-out physical inspection of the property; agents are not going to be checking the water pressure or seeing if the appliances work; rather, they are simply going to get a working idea of what your home is like, good and bad, positive and negative.

Okay, so now the tour of your home is finished; time for the presentation, right? Well, not for me. I think agents, prior to the presentation, need to get inside your head; they need to probe and find out exactly what your needs are. This is a good thing. Without them knowing where you're at mentally, emotionally, and so forth with the upcoming sale of your home, it is going to be difficult for them to ascertain the most appropriate direction you need to go. I typically already have an idea why a particular homeowner is selling prior to the interview, but details are vitally important. Often, these are personal matters the client did not want to discuss on the phone or via e-mail but felt more comfortable doing so in person.

I want to know what my clients *truly* need and want: What is it that is important to them? Everyone is different, and people's needs can go in many different directions. I've had clients who simply wanted to take advantage of what looked like an inflated market, while others' needs were more personal, often *very* personal. For instance, I have had some clients whose spouse or children had very serious health issues that required a change in environment. That sale took on a completely different meaning for both me and my clients. Let agents ask questions; it's important that they are on the same page with you. Okay, *now* we go on to the presentation. Promise!

The Presentation

The presentation should reflect the personality and professionalism of each individual agent. It will either bond you with the person or make you want him or her out of your house as fast as possible! Not necessarily the real estate agent's fault, it's just that we are all different, and you are going to bond or match up to different types of agents and their presentations better than perhaps another homeowner would.

I have certain ways I present our services; I occasionally use some but not a whole lot of bells and whistles, and when I do, they are at the appropriate time. Sometimes, if the situation calls for it, I will use graphs and the such, but in general, I do not. I just can't totally count on them. Everyone's home is unique, and I must take a lot of different things into consideration. There's a time and place for everything, so for the most part, I feel that all too often statistics and graphs can fuzzy people's thinking. Typically I have found the type of presentation that needs graphs and the such are more suitable for perhaps industrial or commercial properties, neither of which Dan or I deal in. Aside from rental property, a house is your home, soon to be another's who may start forming emotional attachments the second he or she steps inside or perhaps even immediately after stepping out of his or her car. Quite frankly, I feel emotions on a large part are what gets my sellers top dollar, which is why adhering to the professionals advice about how to prepare the property to maximize attraction to the buyer is imperative.

Now some home sellers may rather see bells, whistles, and lots and lots of graphs and diagrams; if so, the agent who uses that approach may be the one the homeowner should work with. You need to go with your comfort zone. How long should a presentation be? I think about twenty to thirty minutes, for me anyway. Now remember, this is the agent talking without you asking questions, unless of course, it's for clarification purposes. Anything more than thirty minutes and the yawns start. Trust me; I've seen it. Early on in my career, I thought the more I talked, the more professional I would come off. Not so, the more I talked, the more the homeowner wanted me to *stop talking*!

What are you looking for in the presentation? Obviously, you want to see what this potential agent is bringing to the table. Many agents do the same kind of thing (signs, flyers, MLS, photos, etc.), but what you are looking for is *how* that agent is explaining these things to you. How that agent can bring this more common yet powerful marketing to a new and better level and how it fits in with your particular home and your individual needs. We mentioned this earlier, but it really is so very important: How is that agent taking tried-and-true methods and expanding on them? What makes this agent stand apart from others? Experience? Professionalism? Personality? Is there some kind of marketing he or she is doing that is not the norm? If so, what is it and most importantly *why* is this particular course of action going to work over some of the more proven methods?

This agent may very well have a great point, but he or she needs to be able to explain it to you in a way that makes complete sense.

Let me give you an example. Sometimes depending on the situation, one of our marketing campaigns will be in the form of a huge e-mail campaign to other real estate agents. Thousands and thousands of agents in our particular area will receive an e-mail with a beautiful flyer of our client's home. This is certainly not an ordinary piece of marketing agents do, like the aforementioned multiple listing service. Rather, this is something that goes a bit further and sets us apart from not all but certainly from what many other agents do. This is just an example. Any kind of unique marketing that we think will work for this individual client and their particular home is something that we will want to discuss with them. I don't believe in blanket statements like, "Yes, Mr. and Mrs. Seller, rest assured, we will market your home." What does that even mean? Particulars should be brought up at the appointment.

Aside from the words you are hearing, you need to look for the agent's demeanor. What is the body language telling you? Is the person sitting way back in the chair, as far away from you as possible? Is he or she moved in closer and obviously feeling comfortable with you? Too close? Aside from being very awkward, this could also be a sign that this is an aggressive agent who does not plan on leaving without something signed? What is the tone of voice? Can you hear the person, or do you have to constantly ask to repeat? Overly loud and almost boisterous? Either one of those could be a sign that this agent is not comfortable.

It is *very* difficult to "act" like you are comfortable; even the best sales people in the world may have a challenge with this. So, if you see that the agent *is* indeed interacting with you and in a very comfortable (yet professional) way, then you are onto something good. I do not think the agent should get too comfortable though. If the person ends up sharing a glass of wine with you, starts making silly jokes, and so forth, then do you think you may have run across an amateur agent? I would say, yes, there is a distinct possibility; professional agents are unlikely to have alcohol with their clients, let alone someone who is not even their client yet.

Sure, agents can and really should be somewhat lighthearted and joke around a little. I mean, you do not want someone who is stiff, robotic, and unapproachable, but the pendulum can swing both ways. There is a nice balance that should be achieved between professionalism and comfort; that an outstanding agent will achieve naturally and sincerely. You want to recognize that this agent is truly enjoying engaging with you. If he or she is not being insincere, you will most likely know it; you'll just kind of sense it.

One last comment about the presentation: some homeowners simply do not want one—a presentation, that is. For whatever reason, this is just not "their thing." That is completely acceptable, and when I am confronted with this, I just mold myself to the homeowners' comfort level and expectations. They do not want to see paperwork scattered on their kitchen table; they most certainly *do not* want to see bells and whistles; rather, they just want to talk. They would rather have a nice casual chat and, in doing so, establish whether I am someone they feel as though they can work with. Again, when this happens, my presentation goes back into my briefcase. I lean back comfortably in the chair and proceed to have a nice discussion about their needs, their home, its value, my experience, and so on. I actually enjoy it when this happens!

I would like to point out one type of agent whom you may encounter, and this is who can sometimes be referred to as the bully agent. They're out there. They are going to give you the impression that they are simply not going to leave your home without a signed contract. My opinion? It's okay for agents to be respectfully diligent in their approach, but it *must* be respectful and not in a bully-like manner.

To that point, if agents start pushing too hard or become borderline obnoxious, you should simply tell them that you have no more time to spend and that you have another obligation but that you will be in touch. If, however, agents are polite in their prose to retain your business *and* you feel trusting and comfortable with them *and* they have proven to you their expertise, then go for it. You can hire such agents and sign the listing contract with them. Just don't allow yourself to be pushed into doing something you are uncomfortable with.

Okay, so the presentation is complete. My next subject will be pricing. Again, this is how *I personally* handle myself at interviews; do you see how there is a system in place here? It's there for a reason, mostly to make my clients more at ease and to help convey important ideas and *ideals* to them in a nicely organized fashion. Another agent may have a different approach, and that's okay. What you are looking for is some semblance of a comfortable flow in the way agents present themselves and their services.

Pricing

How long should this take? Again, me? About fifteen to twenty. In most cases, pricing is pretty cut and dry but only if agents have done their— you should know the phrase by now—due diligence! It will be difficult to argue price. Why? Because aside from certain exceptions, it's obvious. Outstanding agents are so prepared they will be able to cut to the chase and give you a narrow range. It's not an exact science, but they should be able to easily give you a well-educated and professional opinion of a low, high, and most probable price your home will sell for.

Where you price it is up to you and can depend on many different determining factors. What are the current market conditions and predictions? How fast do you want to move? Are you facing financial problems that may result in a missed payment on your home? Have you already found a new home? Or are you okay to wait a little and see if you can get a bit higher than market? Whatever the case is, it is your home and your decision not the agent's.

That said, agents do not have to work with you if they are uncomfortable with your pricing, but I think they should never argue with you about it. They can call your attention to certain facts that may educate you, but I do not think they should abruptly attempt to coerce you into listing at the price they want you to list at. True, some homeowners react well to such aggressiveness. I'm just saying I will personally never push price to the point of rudeness to my clients nor would I ever support that type of approach.

I let them know, again, by providing them with hard proof combined with decades of experience what I feel their home is worth. If, however, they are uncomfortable with that figure and feel they can get more, then

I have a decision to make. Generally, I will agree if it's not an overly out-rageous and exaggerated amount they are seeking. But for the most part, homeowners will usually agree that my pricing is appropriate and about what they had in mind anyway. I've gained their trust and showed them facts to help substantiate the price, a very powerful combination by the way, that is—trust and facts. But once again, and—I want to be very clear—I usually have no problem entertaining a higher-than-normal price if it's at least somewhat within the general ball park and not extraordinarily inflated. In some cases, depending on the situation, I will actually suggest asking a price much higher than what the market *seems* to dictate.

In cases like this, for whatever reason, clients simply do not feel their home was worth as much as I thought it was, and again, I literally had to sit there and convince them why I felt they were asking too little. Again, experienced agents have an almost sixth sense where it pertains to real estate value. They often see and feel things that the actual owners just do not; perhaps the owners have been there for decades and take for granted what they have.

Here is an example. This was on a property I was being interviewed to list. It was an older home and had quite a bit of deferred maintenance as older homes quite often do. The owners really felt they would not get as much for the property as what the market was dictating. Evidently other agents agreed with the homeowners' assessment of value. But the home-owners are not the professionals; the agents are.

The homeowners then proceeded to point out a few things about the house including the fact that the old, shabby carpet had been there as long as one could remember. I knew there was more there, but I could certainly understand why the clients did not. But remember, the clients are *not* pro-fessionals in the real estate industry. What *they* saw was *not* what I saw, nor was it what I felt.

As they were again apologizing for the general condition of the prop-erty, I nicely asked if I could have their permission to go into one of the rooms and carefully lift a corner of that carpet up? They were a little con-fused but said, "Sure, why not?" They followed me into the room; I already knew what I was going to find under that carpet but I *did not* know to what degree. As I lifted the carpet, all three of us gazed upon what looked like brand-new hardwood flooring! Of course, it was not brand new; it was even better than that. It was a *very* high quality *vintage* hardwood flooring. Now, this is again where it is essential that an agent understands and keeps up with trends. We happened to be in a market where hardwood flooring, especially vintage, was very high in demand. This flooring did not even need refinishing; it was that perfect. Carpeting must have been laid from the time that property was built and replaced continually without ever having the flooring exposed to harmful factors, be that the elements, the moving around of furniture, kids, pets, and so forth.

This is not the first time I've seen this; I knew what to look for. I knew as we all do, for instance, that children make noise running around a home, and they also increase the risk of injuring themselves if they fall. Now because of that Mom and Dad often just stuck carpet over the floor to both muffle the sound and to keep the kids from getting hurt.

They were elated and just a little embarrassed, but they should not have been. How in the world would they know what to look for? There were a few other things I had discovered in their home that they were not aware of, but for the most part, in this particular example, that old, shaggy carpet help put many, many thousands of dollars right into my very happy home sellers' hands. Needless to say, they listed their home right there and then with me and canceled their next interview. And yes, it is okay to cancel appointments if you are that confident with your new agent. Why put yourself through another long interview when you know you have found the right real estate agent for your purposes?

I have many other examples of this sort of thing happening, but my point is, do not underestimate years of experience and the professional's sixth sense about certain things, whether that professional is your plumber, doctor, or yes, your real estate agent. Whatever the case, if I feel my clients can get more than what they think or even more than what other agents are telling them, I will be very forthright in my opinions, but again, whether it is asking higher or lower, it is the clients' home, and the final decision is theirs. Whatever city and state you reside in, I'm quite confident there are agents out there who know how to do this type of thing *and* know your particular area's market and trends. This, of course, should result in you getting the best price possible for your home.

Now, let's look at the flip side of this situation: say, homeowners have a very exaggerated idea of what their home is worth, so unbelievable and out of reality that most agents would pass. There are still some agents who simply do not care about grossly overpricing homes; they will list a property at any price. Why? Because some (not all) of them may be thinking, "There is no way this house is going to sell at this price, but hey, eventually this seller will get discouraged and lower the price, and then I'll make my commission." Now ask yourself, is that honest or professional? Of course, it is not.

Here's something else to consider. Some agents are okay to list your home at an outrageous price even if your home never sells. Why? Because all the time you have it on the market, they might be picking up new clients, new buyers, or even sellers who called them off the sign, an ad, or perhaps an open house; it's called exposure, and in a sense, your over-priced home is bait to catch new business. I would like to believe that most agents do not handle themselves in this fashion, but the unfortunate truth is that some of them do. Just be aware.

I've seen home sellers really hurt themselves with pricing. There are two terms I use in situations such as these because they're so appropriate. First, "shop worn." A house can get "shop worn" very easily and faster than you may think. I also use the analogy "The new kid on the block." When your home first goes on the market, it really is "the new kid on the block"; everyone's looking. They're all excited about meeting this new kid, but then before you know it, another new kid joins the community; now you are old news.

What is worse, new buyers (and there are always new buyers coming on the scene) will see that the home has been on the market for quite some time. "Hmm," they may ask, "why have a bunch of other homes sold, but this one hasn't? Is there something wrong with the owner? Are they difficult people to deal with? Is the agent difficult? Do I really want to involve myself in a transaction with them?" And it's not just the buyers; the agents can also become suspicious. The *absolute* worst question buyers can possibly ask is this: "Is there something wrong with this house?" They may think that is the reason it has not sold and other homes have when in fact that is not the case at all.

Being on the market too long compared with other similar homes can be very dangerous territory. I would encourage you, if you trust the agent you chose, to try to adhere to their advice, at least within reason. Now, you may be thinking, "Well the buyer is not going to think there is anything wrong with my home; they are just going to assume it has not sold because the price was too high." Well, yes and no. Let's say you put your property on the market for an overly high price; two months go by, and nothing, so you lower the price. Now that buyer is probably only going to see that adjusted lower price and how long it has been on the market. There's a chance they will not know the price was ever higher, so they might think that it has always been at that price, which will in turn raise the question: "At that price why has this property been on the market that long? Is there something wrong with this house?" True, there are reports or part of the listing that buyers can sometimes see that will show that indeed the price was much higher at one time, but truthfully, they are probably not going to pay that much attention to it. Ordinarily, I have found that buyers' attention spans are pretty short on things like this; they will just go on to the next listing for sale.

Chapter Conclusion

So now you have listened to the presentation and you have heard the pricing; what's next? Now it's your turn; the spotlight is on you. This is your opportunity to ask questions and get more clarification on things that were in the presentation or in the pricing. Just refer back to the "Questions" section of this chapter and if you have your own questions by all means ask them.

After your question-and-answer session, that is (for me anyway) the end of the interview. If the client feels comfortable and confident enough to proceed to hire me and establish an agent-client relationship, then we move forward right there and then and sign the listing paperwork even if the client has another interview or two. But that said, if the client feels as though they need a little more time to think about things or still wants to go through with those other interviews, then I understand. What I will typically do is schedule a follow-up appointment to meet with them again.

I will say, however, that I do not think there is ever a full 100 percent knowing that the correct decision is being made. I mean, I think that goes for just about anything in life, but if the feeling is solid enough that you just kind of know inside that there is a very strong likelihood you are making the correct decision, then it is my opinion to move forward. If you do not act from this place of knowing what can sometimes happen is that you put your mind on overload by overthinking things; now that might have an opposite and negative affect that will put you in a position of not being able to make *any* choice. I believe they call that paralysis by analysis, but we are getting a bit too much into psychology here! Just go with your instinct, and you'll be fine.

I hope I've been able to help you by walking you through this process. I've had the pleasure of working with many very happy and satisfied clients, and my wish for you is that you will find an agent who brings the home-selling process to a higher level of ease and professionalism. I sincerely hope sharing some of my experience has helped you!

"In any moment of decision, the best thing you can do is the right thing, the next best thing is the wrong thing, and the worst thing you can do is nothing."

—Theodore Roosevelt

5

MAKING YOUR FINAL DECISION

So, that's it; you're done with the entire hiring process except for, well, hiring someone! You'll be wondering, "What now? Who did the best job? Who did I like the most? Who has the most experience? Who understands best and is most experienced with my particular situation?"

The Early Decision
Like Joy mentioned, there is a strong possibility that, because you prepared and selected well, you will feel a healthy connection with one of the agents and will want to start the process. That's great, and that is the goal of this book, to find the ideal agent and proceed to get your home sold for a fantastic price with great service. This may even happen at your first or second interview. If you feel that confident then it would be my recommendation to just move forward and cancel your other appointments, or you can even ask your new agent to contact those agents on your behalf and let them know that you have already made a decision. If, however, you just do not feel that, then I might not recommend making any commitments or choices at this particular juncture. Maybe just give it a little time; let everything sink in for a bit. I'd like to give you some guidance on how to make this process as easy on yourself as possible.

Making a Decision at the Final Interview

Sometimes what happens is that homeowners are so worn out by the final interview of the day that they just list with the last agent they've met even though they'd thought the first or second agent was the right choice. This does happen. Don't do this to yourself; you are tired and worn out. I understand this; although it does not have to be, often the process can be very draining. You just want to be done with it. However, you will only hurt yourself more in the long run by signing with someone who would not have been your number-one pick.

Making a Virtual Decision

In the old days if you did not hire an agent that day, then you had to make another appointment to have them come back out. Another couple of hours, time out of your day, and time away from things you should or would like to be doing, like preparing to make a move! Here is where technology can really help you. Why does that agent even have to come back out? They certainly will if you want them to. I know that Joy personally enjoys and is excited about returning to visit with our new clients, once they've decided to use us as their real estate agents. But here it is: the agent does not have to come back out. The listing contract can simply be e-mailed to you, all nicely highlighted where you need to sign and initial. You print it out; do your signatures; and scan, fax, or mail it right back to the agent, all in a matter of minutes.

There are also electronic signatures like DocuSign, a very fast, simple, and reliable way to obtain electronic signatures. As long as this is acceptable with your agent's brokerage, you can electronically sign your name—no printing or scanning—quick and easy, and you're done. Anyone can do it; you do not need to sign up for anything. It's literally a process of a few minutes. Even if you believe you are not that computer savvy, this one is a piece of cake. But...are you more traditional? No problem. The initial listing contract is not that big; it can be faxed to you, and you can fax it back, or it can simply be sent in regular mail with a stamped self-addressed envelope. But again, this is only if time or desire does not permit you to have the agent come back out. This is entirely your call; most agents have no problem coming back out, as I said earlier. Joy actually prefers it; we are both excited and happy to start working with our new clients face to face.

Making No Decision

If you find yourself just a bit overwhelmed and a little confused on who to pick, then you did the right thing by holding off. But now, how do you eliminate all this confusion and indecision. Well, there may be a chance that you were not impressed with any of them; there's nothing wrong with that, and you will need to go back to the drawing board. However, I do not think that will happen; I suspect you are going to favor at least one of the agents you interviewed. Why? Because you did your homework before you even let them in your home; you were already a little comfortable with them all, before you even met them. You just now need to find out who you are *a lot* comfortable with— And you must be more than just *comfortable* with them. Just make sure that comfortable has companions like professionalism, confidence, experience, skills, and reputation in the real estate industry. When you recognize this in one particular agent, then I think your indecision will more easily turn into a final decision.

Salespersons

I'd like to address some things for you to think about after your interview that may help this decision making easier. Remember you interviewed a real estate salesperson. They are in a service *and* sales business. Although there are exceptions, for the most part, I think they would not be in this industry if they did not like people and enjoyed engaging in talk. But this could be a double-edged sword (does not have to be but could). Some agents are very proficient at presenting themselves even though they may lack experience or even lack the specialty needed for a certain sale. They still can get hired. Why? Because the homeowner did not recognize a sales pitch. This could have been very innocent on the agents' part. As long as the client was not misled, the agent, for whatever reason, perhaps just lots of personality, was able to get hired by talking the homeowner into utilizing his or her services even with little experience and know-how. We can all get caught up in certain charismas easier than we think. Many agents in the real estate industry can be extremely likeable people. Just be aware.

Be on guard that there is the "other" type of salesperson and not the nice type. Keep in mind, not all salespersons like people; some downright dislike others, but for whatever reason, they have a skill to sell. We can all buy into their perceived likeablity. Charisma and charm are fine as long as they're not accompanied by lies and deception. That type of salesperson is for sure out there, so do be aware.

But back to what we hope is the nice type of salesperson. I know that some homeowners might be attracted to certain personality traits or the fact that they may have something in common, even though the agent is clearly not qualified. We've occasionally been on the losing side of this kind of thing. There have been a few times when Joy was interviewed for the job of selling a home and lost out to someone else who I knew had nowhere near our qualifications or for that matter perhaps even the qualifications of any of the other agents the homeowner had interviewed.

Aside from natural and normal disappointment on these occasions, I would also be disappointed that there was a strong likelihood our would-be client was going to have a miserable experience, and this, of course, would end up hurting not only them but also reflecting adversely on our industry as a whole.

Let me share a couple of stories to give you an idea of what I mean. Every agent, no matter his or her level of production has been in similar situations.

Would-Be Client

> *Hi, Dan and Joy, we'd decided to list with you guys. That is, until we just happened to run into another real estate agent at a party Saturday night; we got to talking about, of all things, politics, and you know, they agreed 100 percent with everything we believe is politically wrong with this country (yeah, right—major sales job!). It was almost like talking to a mirror; that's how much we agreed with each other! Anyway, well, sorry, Dan and Joy.*

Would-Be Client

Joy, you are awesome; I am so impressed with not only you but with the Blanding Team as a whole that I plan on telling everyone I know about you. You guys rock! However, I listed with another agent. We did not know each other, but I found out he actually went to the same high school as me. We just got talking about the old alma mater and some mutual students we knew, and, well, I just listed with him... Sorry.

Okay. FYI, on this last one, I checked the experience factor on this quasi high-school old-friend agent: virtually nothing. Worse, I believe he may have been a part-timer.

Now were any of the two agents deceptive in their presentation or did they withhold information that I think the client deserved to know—like *I'm a part-time agent!*—I will never know. Once a client signs with another brokerage, depending on the contract, I have an ethical obligation to no longer communicate with them, aside from returning their call or e-mail if asked, regarding their decision. I would only hope that in most of these cases at least it was the inexperienced but honest salesperson agent rather than the other type, but I fear that is not always the case.

Trust—a Worn and Overused Word?

Let's for a moment address the word "trust" in a little more depth. It is painfully obvious that it can be an overused word in many sales fields, and that can sometimes of course include the real estate industry. I think we have all heard the phrase that goes something along the lines of, "If a salesman tells you to trust him, run!" There is a lot of truth to that, and let me give you an example to help drive home my point.

If someone you really do not know comes up to you and tells you to give him or her twenty dollars, are you going to do it? I suspect not. Why? There is no reason to; this person has given you absolutely nothing that will substantiate any justification whatsoever for giving him or her the twenty dollars. So, you walk away, or sure maybe even run!

Now let's say another person approached you that you still really did not know, but you *did* know he or she had a very good reputation over the years as being a very kind philanthropist and that the person even had things—for instance, like a website—showing many of the charitable organizations he or she was involved with. Maybe this person even specialized in one particular charity that was very dear to your heart. Now, would you give this person the twenty dollars? Perhaps yes, maybe no, but I bet you would probably at least consider it. I doubt you would walk away, and for sure, I don't think you would run. Why? Because he or she has something the other person did not have. Reputation, experience, and the facts to support them.

That is kind of how I want you to embrace the term "trust." Certainly not blindly; rather, a very well thought out decision based on facts combined with an inner feeling. I really think that is the safest approach to take. Will you ever be 100 percent sure you can trust this person that you do not know that well? Probably not, I don't think any decision on hiring someone can be 100 percent. An employer can hire a new employee based on all the reasons we have talked about: facts, skills in a certain specialty the employer needs, experience, reputation, and so forth, but can that employer be absolutely 100 percent sure it is the right pick? I would say it is unlikely, but he or she can certainly put the odds well in his or her favor. I want you to think on those same lines.

But what if you are on the fence about a choice? Two agents, so perfect for the job, but you just don't know which way to go, and you really do trust them both. This is where you have to dig inside a bit. If, for whatever reason, your gut trust level was even a little higher for one agent over the other, *and* this agent possessed the skills you need for your particular situation, then I would suggest going that route. I am highly confident you will be happy with your choice. The word "trust" can still carry strength and goodwill if it is presented properly.

How to Break the News to the Other Agents
Okay, you know who you want; there is little to no questions about it. Whew! You made your decision; you called your new agent. You're happy,

the agent's happy, and you have a great feeling about your choice. Now you need to tell the other agents. You may think, " do I really have to? Just when I was finally feeling like the pressure is off now, I have to, in a sense, tell would-be employees that they didn't get the job. Ugh!" Here are some thoughts and ideas on how to make this simpler. First, yes you probably should tell them, but in the end, that is your call.

When to Tell Them?
Immediately—that is, immediately *after* you have signed a listing contract. You can, but if you do it prior to that, you run the risk of the particular agent hounding you to change your mind; don't put yourself through that. That's why I prefer you telling them after you sign a contract with another agent. Depending on the contract, once the property is listed, it could be inappropriate and unethical for other agents to have further contact with you.

How to Tell Them
I would recommend e-mail communication. Direct phone contact, although more personal, can also be extremely awkward. Do you really want to talk to this person directly? I suspect not, and truthfully that agent will most probably not want to talk to you. It's nothing really personal, or should not be anyway; it's just that it can just be so darn uncomfortable for both parties.

It comes down to your choice. I see no reason a phone call needs to be made in such situations. But there are exceptions. If it's a friend or family member (again, it's been our experience that using such persons to sell your home could be a big mistake), then a phone call might be appropriate. If it's an agent you have used before or an agent you do have some sort of relationship with, then you may consider the phone call. Really, it's a case-by-case judgment call on your part.

What to Tell Them
Keep it brief and simple; compliment them (if deserved), but I would suggest not going overboard with that. With too many compliments, the agent

may get confused and truthfully a bit frustrated as to why you did not choose them if they were such a great agent. Something like this should suffice:

> *Thank you so much for all your efforts and professionalism you displayed when we met last Saturday. I have made a decision to utilize the services of another agent. Thank you again, and I sincerely wish you the best of good fortune in all your business endeavors.*
>
> *Sincerely,*
> *Jane*

Okay, as you can see, this is short, professional, and to the point. You can mix it up anyway you like to fit your personality, but this at least gives you a working idea. If you felt the agent was unprofessional or did not show appropriate efforts, then simply leave that part out.

Their Response
Keep in mind, because of your earnestness in the interview process, all your potential candidates were professional; we hope anyway. If you get any kind of nasty or ill-meant response, you have then just proven to yourself that you most certainly made the right choice.

I suspect for the most part you will simply get no response. I would like to add one last thing, and that is some agents may ask why: "Why not me and why the other agent?" This is an appropriate question. Many agents are simply trying to improve themselves, which is admirable. It may sting a bit for them to hear the reason, but you'll be helping them in the long run.

Okay, there you go; the process is complete, and you will have hired the perfect real estate agent for the job of selling your home and for top dollar! I could end this book right here, but I felt it would be too abrupt of an end. You listed your home with an outstanding real estate agent, but now another journey is just beginning.

"The reward of a thing well done is to have done it."

—*Ralph Waldo Emerson*

6

YOU'VE HIRED AN AGENT FOR THE JOB OF SELLING YOUR HOME; WHAT NOW?

Everything is in order. You have successfully hired an agent. Now it's time to move forward. Before I address some of the stages you will be going through with your agent, I want to talk briefly about one element that is truly the proverbial glue that is holding everything together, and that is *proper* communication.

Communication

I do not think there is any worse feeling a seller can experience than being sold to utilize the service of a particular agent only to have that agent all but abandon them after the listing contract has been signed. This happens all too often in our industry and perhaps more often than you may realize. This is one of the reasons we put in place a very strict communication schedule; under no circumstances would I want *our* clients thinking even for one second that they are being ignored or that the business they gave us is being taken for granted.

I am just amazed at how a homeowner can hire an agent to sell their home and then accept silence. You should never accept a lack of communication. If agents do not do what they promised at the interview, then you have every right and really a duty as the seller of your home to call them up on it. Make sure agents adequately communicate with you and do what they assured you they would.

I would not recommend being too aggressive with them, at first anyway. You are at this point just clarifying a few things, that's all. Simply tell them that you thought you recalled at their presentation that they said they would be doing so and so and that you don't see that happening. An outstanding agent (Remember, no agent is perfect, even an outstanding one) will agree, immediately apologize, proceed to fix the problem, and never let it happen again. If, however, you get no change in their service, then being a little more aggressive and demanding may be appropriate. I really hope that since you went through the proper steps to hire the right agent that this does not become an issue, but the truth is it can, and if so, it must be brought to the agent's attention.

As articulated earlier in this book, agents must have some sort of system to communicate. If they just call you on a whim or are simply returning your call, you will not be comfortable; rather, you will tend to be nervous, wondering, "What is happening with the sale of my home?" or "Why have there been no offers yet?" You may be even asking yourself, "Am I, as the homeowner, doing something wrong?" These are questions you should *never* have to ask yourself!

An outstanding agent can usually address these and all issues before they're even a thought in your head. That is why we found it so important to have certain days to communicate with our clients. This gives the client reassurance, knowing that, aside from certain exceptions, they will for sure be getting communication like clockwork.

Now that I have made it very clear that follow-up and communication after you have entered into a contract are imperative, I'd like to take you through four stages of what will be happening from the time your home goes on the market to the day it closes escrow and beyond. They are as follows:

- while on the open market,
- negotiating offers,
- the closing process, and
- the actual move and your agents after close follow-up.

While on the Open Market

It has been my experience that while you are on the market, agents need to be very proactive. They cannot sit back and wait for an offer. The behind-the-scenes work is very important. I will sum up this phase with what I call the "Big four." The four most critical elements that an agent must be able to not only successfully perform but, equally important, successfully communicate to you are as follows:

- market knowledge,
- other agents' inputs,
- buyer behavior, and
- your immediate neighborhood.

Market Knowledge

Assuming agents are doing everything they promised you with regard to marketing and you have still not had an acceptable offer within a reasonable time frame, then they absolutely must share market updates with you; I cannot emphasize enough how unbelievably important this is. As a matter of fact, I think, in general, market updates should happen immediately after a property has been listed; that is how important it is.

Let's say, as an example, that homes are selling so-so, but they are beginning to take longer than normal. The last thing you would want your agent to say to you after not having heard from him or her for a while is this: "Um, Mr. and Mrs. Homeowner, it has been a while since we listed your property, and I think your home went down in value, like a lot!"

That is for sure not a competent agent; what you should have heard is something like this: "Mr. and Mrs. Seller, as you have seen from my weekly market updates, it is obvious there are signs that a downward shift in value is beginning to happen. I would suggest perhaps we adjust the price a little before our competition does to avoid getting caught up in a downward spiral."

Do you see the obvious difference? That first agent waited too long; he or she simply did not do their research and analysis. That agent should have been studying trends in the market and sharing it with the client on a *very* regular basis. Instead, while he or she was doing nothing, the market slowly turned downward right under the agent's nose. Unfortunately, through no fault of the owners, by the time they found out, it was too late; the home could not be sold for anywhere near what it could have been sold for had this downward trend of depreciation been spotted earlier.

The skillful agent was more like a hawk, carefully watching, studying, and learning about what was happening in the marketplace, not just local, but state, national, and even worldwide. This agent caught on very early that a negative change was beginning to emerge and subsequently was able to still get his or her client a great price while many of the client's neighbors sat on the market unsuspectingly losing money daily.

Other Agents' Inputs

I have never met homeowners who did not love compliments about their property; who wouldn't? A home holds a very special place in most owners' hearts, but if homeowners are truly serious about selling and for the best price possible, perhaps compliments are not what they need. What good are nice words about a home you are trying to sell when in the end the person with the flattery has no interest in buying it? If ever you needed brutal honesty, it is now. Don't get me wrong; compliments can be good but only if they walk hand in hand with constructive criticism.

Your agent should be telling you what other agents are saying about your house both positive *and* negative. Some uncomfortable things may need to be said, like "The beds were not made" or "The bathroom was a wreck!" or "There were dirty dishes stacked a mile high in the kitchen" or worse comments. Yes, very difficult to hear, but it is imperative they are brought to attention and dealt with to get the best price possible for your home.

Buyer Behavior

How many buyers are inquiring about your property? A home seller may ask, "Does it really matter if they are not making an offer anyway?" It truly does matter. The agent and you both need to have a close pulse on the market week by week. Many things can affect value, both positively and negatively. If we know a certain amount of buyers have been inquiring about your home but to no successful end, then there may be some problems. What is it that is stopping these buyers dead in their tracks from wanting to see your property, let alone making an offer on it? You need to know the answers to these types of questions.

Your Immediate Neighborhood

What has been happening in your neighborhood? Did another home like yours just go on the market? Your agent has to know these things and share them with you. *In order to sell a home successfully*—and I cannot stress this point enough—your agent needs to watch your immediate neighborhood very, very closely. Competition is a very real thing when it comes to home sales. Any good businessperson will always try to stay one step ahead of the competition.

So, there you have the big four. They are extremely important, so much so that I would urge you to refer back to this section repeatedly if necessary.

Negotiating Offers

This should be an exciting and positive part of the process. Certain things were performed by both you and the agent that resulted in someone wanting to buy your house. Think about it: this is a very favorable accomplishment for both of you. I will not get into details about the logistics of offer negotiating. It can be very complex. Each agent has a different strategy and approach to the process. Unless you have reason to question your agent's service and integrity, then think about it: he or she has gotten you this far, gained your confidence to be hired in the first place, and has been professionally communicating with you. Efforts resulted in getting an offer on your property. Whatever your agent said or did, it got the results you were looking for, an offer. So based on this success thus far, why not just trust the person to continue to work in the same appropriate manner to negotiate the best price and terms possible, and let's address this word, "terms," for a moment. Many sellers have a tendency, and understandably so, to look at the dollar amount and nothing else. This can be dangerous territory. Questions need to be asked, and documentation needs to be provided: Can this buyer truly qualify to purchase your home? Does the person have sufficient funds in the bank? and so forth. Again, if you've trusted your agent thus far, then I think you should consider that faith into the negotiating stage.

Homeowners generally do not understand "the art" of negotiating where it pertains to real estate. This is not like selling an automobile; this will be someone's home. Houses are very expensive; buyers are often very nervous and emotional. Your real estate agent needs to understand the psychology behind buying a home and in doing so better represent you by keeping everyone calm. This is the reason, and I mentioned this earlier, that it is so important your agent has years of experience working with buyers. That knowledge both logistically and psychologically is going to give that agent a huge edge in skillfully making sure you get the best price and terms possible for your home.

The Closing Process

This could very well be, in my opinion, where your agent is really earning that commission. Now that a deal has been consummated, there is yet another wave of new challenges that falls into the lap of your agent, and that is to obtain a successful close of escrow.

In the closing process having a discerning agent looking over everything is critical. We have used this terminology before in this book, but it's just so very appropriate: there are so many moving parts in the closing process of a house. What happens behind the scenes in the closing of a home can be quite complicated and could be overwhelming, and that is an understatement, to someone who is not familiar with the real estate sales process. This process needs to be treated in a manner similar to the marketing process. Your agent should be in touch with you on a regular basis. Will there be issues or hiccups? Yes, likely. There is a lot going on, and probably a couple dozen or more entities, people, and individual personalities involved, so yes, there will likely be challenges. That is why earlier in the book I mentioned that one of the worst agents is the "nervous" one. That is because they can spread panic to everyone involved in the transaction: the buyer, the buyer's agent, the closing office, the contractors, and so forth—most importantly, you.

As you have found in this chapter, if the agent is calm and communicative, then these "problems" will not seem so dire, and really for the most part, they're not that dire; they are just things that sometimes happen during the closing process of a home, simple as that. Nothing to get too worried or too stressed over. If you chose the right agent, then you picked someone who can be calm and in control in all situations, which will almost always result in relatively smooth sailing during your closing process. That said, sometimes the sailing is anything but smooth, and you may find yourself becoming upset with your agent.

Remember all those "moving parts" that were repeated throughout this book? Well, because there are so many of them—moving parts, that is—frustrations, confusions, and yes, downright irritations are bound to happen. We mentioned earlier that there are probably a couple dozen or so entities and individuals involved in a real estate transaction. Those individuals…they all have their own personalities and idiosyncrasies, dilemmas, and complications are going to happen, and you may feel a need to blame your agent.

Sometimes it will indeed be your agent's fault. Like I have mentioned a few times, no one is perfect; the superhero outstanding agent is simply nonexistent. Human error and miscommunications may happen during the process of working with all those "moving parts." Know this, and if you are upset with your agent, for goodness sake, tell him or her because if you do not, that anger or even that slight irritation is not going to go away. Rather, it will linger, and then when another problem comes up, even one that is in no way your agent's fault, you are going to get even more upset. That anger might get directed straight toward your agent, thus putting an unnecessary strain on the relationship. I really want to see you try to avoid that.

If you trust your real estate agent, and you should, if you used the techniques outlined in this book, then trust that you can be honest with him or her. I would much rather have a client call or even e-mail me and tell me they're feeling a little frustration toward me than say nothing at all. At least then I can address it, and if it is my fault, admit it, apologize for it, fix it, and never let it happen again. If it had nothing to do with me...well, I would tell my client that and then proceed to investigate the source where it originated and pursue trying to get it resolved.

If your agent admits fault, forgive, and move on. If the problem truly had nothing to do with the agent, then believe him or her and have confidence that the agent is doing everything in his or her power to address the difficulty and overcome it. Conversely, if you are particularly happy about something(s) your agent did, then tell the person that. Everyone, and I mean *everyone*, can use a compliment every now and then! All healthy relationships have two things in common: honesty and communication; a real estate agent–client relationship is certainly no different.

The Actual Move and Your Agents after Close Follow-Up

The agent-client relationship is more than a fiduciary ethical relationship between the two; it is also a human relationship during a very stressful period of your life.

Your real estate agent's conduct during the selling process, from the time you list your home with him or her to the day it closes escrow, will directly affect your experience during the actual move and relocation.

This is very important, so I will repeat: Your real estate agent's conduct during the selling process, from the time you list your home with him or her to the day it closes escrow, will directly affect your experience during the actual move and relocation.

If your agent was professional and also emotionally supportive and empathetic during the listing and selling period, the actual physical move and relocation will be much easier on you. Conversely, if you hired an agent who ended up being less than professional, you will see that neglect reflected adversely in the move and relocation. I don't want you to discover the importance of this very significant agent/client relationship *after the fact*. I want you to understand it now, before you hire your real estate agent.

Try getting online sometime, and look up stressful life events. I'm confident you will find "moving" in your searches. Moving is tough; how could it not be? There is so much going on during an extremely short period of time.

Let's take a quick look at just a few challenges, starting with more of the minor ones up to some very serious challenges. Now remember, this is just moving without any other external stress factors involved, and again we are starting with just the more mild irritants.

Packing

I will tell you this from lots of and lots of experience with home sellers as well as from personal experience. You almost always have more "stuff" than you think. What do you keep? What do you throw away? Gathering up the boxes, carefully wrapping up your household and personal items— tedious, time consuming, and sometimes downright irritating. The move is almost always much more intense then you originally thought.

Utility Companies

Seems easy enough, right? Well, you would think, but sometimes things go awry; miscommunications on dates to turn off and turn on can sometimes creep into what should be a simple request. Not a huge stressor, more of a minor headache than anything, but a headache all the same.

Cleaning

For the most part, I have found homeowners do like to leave their home in at least a somewhat clean condition. This is not like your normal weekly cleaning. You find dirt and cobwebs in even the most obsessively clean homes. They just kind of appear, resulting in the cleaning project becoming much greater than you had originally anticipated and planned for. This is not a huge stressor, but it is adding one more element to the mix that can cause some anxiety.

Relocating Children

Okay, now it is getting a bit more serious, isn't it? If your move involves kids, you are going to have to deal with their emotions, leaving neighborhood friends and classmates, and the fear they may feel starting new in another school, another neighborhood, and so forth. Sometimes that house is all those children ever knew, and they are having to deal with their own little emotions about that.

Leaving Your Community, Neighbors, Friends and Family
A move often brings with it a severing of ties that can be tough. Although, sometimes depending on the situation, it could be a big relief getting away from certain people (like nosy neighbors!), often, however, it is not that way. Sure you say, "you'll stay in touch," but will you? Hopefully yes with your family but the others? Maybe, but we all know there is a chance that you may not. It can be downright sad leaving neighbors, friends, family and familiar connections.

Facing an Unknown Community
If you are fortunate enough, you may be very familiar with where you are going, but even if you are, you really don't know the finer details until you have been there awhile. But what if you are not familiar, that is, with your new community? Can that be a little frightening? Of course! How could it not? You are leaving your comfort zone and doing something a lot of people *do not* like to do, even if it is positive, and that is *change*.

The list could go on, but you get my point. These are just normal ordeals *anyone* would have to face with a move, no matter what the situation is. In the absolute best of circumstances, these still must be dealt with. Sure, perhaps you can contract people to take care of some of these things for you; that will ease off the pressure—well, a little anyway—but you are still going to have to deal with them on some level; there is really no getting around it. One last thing I would like to bring to your attention: all this is happening immediately on the heels of you having gone through what is usually a somewhat lengthy and stressful selling and closing process.

I am certainly not trying to alarm you or for that matter discourage you from making a move, but rather, I am attempting to bring to light the intensity of what you will be doing. Many, if not most, homeowners are not taking this into consideration when they are hiring an agent. If they did, they would be so very much more careful in the process. That agent is going to be dealing with you very closely and knowing that the person is empathetic and emotionally supportive to the stressors you will be enduring is, in my opinion, of the upmost importance. An agent who is looking for their payday and nothing else? Hey, even if he or she did a splendid job selling your home, getting you a great price, great terms, and a smooth enough escrow, that is simply not enough.

Professionals need to remind themselves constantly of what you are going through. That is not to say that agents should get too attached; no professional would because it will adversely affect their duties for all their clients including you. But they need to still, at the very minimum, be conscious and sensitive for what you are or will be experiencing.

We already took a look at the actual move and some of the difficult elements involved. So, let's now look at some of the reasons you might be moving. These reasons can range from exciting to downright terrifying. Let's look at a few, and we will start with some of the more positive ones.

Moving to Purchase Another Home
This is typically a favorable move, but here again, you now have two situations going on at the same time: the sale of your home and the purchase. A double whammy, especially if the move is going to require interim housing. Although for the large part we are able to avoid our clients having to go through two moves, sometimes there is simply no choice. If we are looking at two moves, then you will have two packing events, two hiring of movers, two dealings with utility companies, and so forth. Again, this should be a positive, exciting event, but it is still, in a word, *overwhelming*. The move just got twice as hard.

Marriage or Any Type of New Cohabitations
This is and should be very exciting. For whatever reason, marriage or otherwise, two people are starting new lives together, under the same house. A little scary? Some apprehension? Yep. Here is another little potential hiccup. Stuff. Whose stuff is going to be kept and whose is going to be discarded or given away? That, of course, is just one example of some of

the difficulties with this life change. This is walking hand in hand with the move.

Retirement: Sounds Exciting, Right?

Well, it is, or at least, it should be, but not unlike two people who are starting a life together—there are a lot of unknowns. The lifestyle the retiring person, as would be the case with their significant other, is accustomed to is running into a very abrupt change. This typically does not happen a little at a time; it could, but I think for the most part, retirement is working one day and not working the next. You can plan for what you are going to do, but until you are actually out there doing it...it will be an unknown, and unknowns can frighten the toughest of persons—this...and still having to deal with the move.

New Job

For whatever reason you are having a career change or a job relocation, that can be very exciting, but it can also be taking you out of the area and into an occupation with new surroundings, new employees, perhaps new coworkers or a new boss, new systems that you will need to learn, training, and so forth—all this...*and* the move.

Divorce or Separation

Okay, now we are going in a different direction; the motivation for the move is not a merry one—it is not an exciting event. Well, it could be depending on how you look at it, but for the most part we are talking about a reason for selling that is way, way up there on the stress level ladder—shattered dreams, unknown future and probably an array of mixed emotions. All these highly intense feelings...sure, it will get better if you want it to, but for now, this intensity is side by side with the other challenges of the move.

Foreclosure

Even if you found that perfect agent who came in and saved the day, stopped a foreclosure and got you money you may have lost, it is still the loss of a home. A broken dream? Oh, you bet. I have sold so very many homes that were in foreclosure, and although I have been witness to things happening for a reason, and I've seen a lot of good come out of such scenarios as this, the truth of the matter is now, as it is happening, it can be devastating to the owners. Remember, that home was originally purchased with a high level of excitement and hope—a huge investment financially and emotionally, pride of ownership, and so forth. Now the reason for you having to sell is literally in your face during the move.

Death
Probably number one on the stress list. That is why I put it last. This homeowner is feeling some unimaginable pain, and the house? Well, it often holds lots of memories for the one left behind. His or her loved one is gone, and now the person is having to leave the home the couple shared their lives with. Or perhaps this property was inherited and this seller had just lost his or her last parent. Lots of grief and perhaps lots of reminders of childhood as the person empties out the house he or she grew up in. Things will get better, but right now? I think "overwhelming" would be an understatement.

Chapter Conclusion
For an agent to not have compassion and understanding in situations such as these in my opinion is just sad. Moving is not easy; I think I made that clear enough, but now throw in any of the above life events or sometimes multiple ones all happening at the same time, and you are being put in a very vulnerable position. Think about that vulnerability, and now think about an agent who did a lousy job selling your home. The property took months more to sell than the agent originally told you and when it did sell...nothing but problems. Things came up during discovery that should have been addressed way, way back when the agent first went into a contract with you. Perhaps the deal completely fell apart, and you had to start the whole process all over again. Your agent rarely returned your calls and sometimes...well, sometimes when he or she spoke to you, it was like you were bothering the person. Let's say you had *that* type of real estate agent

or worse. Will that make a difference in the pressures you have to deal with in the actual move and relocation? Of course, it will.

Let's take a look at this from another angle. You put forth appropriate measures to hire an agent you really thought would represent you well, and the agent not only did that but also exceeded your expectations. That is not to say the agent was perfect, but you know he or she always had your best interests at heart. Escrow is closed; Yes, it was a little bumpy, but you know all real estate transactions can have a little turbulence, but in this case, your agent was like that confident, trustworthy pilot and brought you through the turbulence to a nice, safe landing.

Now everything is behind you, and you are having to go through the move. No, the agent is not there at the house helping you pack, but you knew he or she was there when it counted. You also know that you could call the agent right now, right smack in the middle of your move, and he or she would return your call promptly, as always. Perhaps you just need to vent a little and yell, "I hate moving!" The agent agrees and gives you a few words of encouragement. Nothing huge, not a full-on motivational speech or pep talk but rather just a few minutes of listening, understanding, and telling you that this *will* end—the move, that is—and that you will get settled down, and life will go back to normal. Just a few words, that's all it takes.

Choose well; prepare yourself for a bit of a ride, but always, always tell yourself, "This will eventually be over; there is an end to this, and when that happens I'm going to sit down, close my eyes for a moment, take a nice sigh of relief, and relax!"

I will end this section with this thought: although your real estate agent has completed the job and successfully delivered what he or she was hired to do does not mean the person should grab the check and never be heard from again. Rather, I think the agent or even a member of the team should stay in touch with you for an appropriate period of time during and after your move, just to ensure you are okay. Remember, you have been working very closely with them; there is a certain bond that was (or should have been) created.

It works both ways; remember, many agents partly got into this business because they sincerely like people. There is no reason why the bond created between you and your real estate agent should be broken at the close of a transaction. Personally, we are in touch with many of our past clients, even clients from decades ago. Every now and again, we will touch base, say, "Hi," and talk about the "good old days" when they were selling their home with us!

If you heeded the advice in this book and ended up *having a successful selling experience, congratulations and great job!* Like in any industry, the business of selling homes is no different and can carry with it accomplishments and accolades along with the unfortunate ill feelings that can be the result of poor representation. Often bad and ugly agents lower the reputation for everyone. Joy and I as well as many other agents have done our best to try to counteract this unfortunate reality. I would urge you to help us with that.

If you have had a wonderful experience with an agent, tell people that. Share the success story; this is not to give that agent free advertisement. As a matter of fact, don't even mention the agent's name if you don't want to (although I'm sure it would be appreciated!), but do let others know that there are indeed competent, honest, and professional agents out there.

I hope the words in this book that have come from our vast experience will help you in the process of choosing the perfect real estate agent!

If you are considering selling your home, please check out the very last couple of pages of this book, titled "Final Note from the Author and Contact Information."

In the meantime, *make good* (no…*make outstanding*) decisions!

SOME COMMON REAL ESTATE TERMS

Real estate agents have a language of their own; some people understand it, or some of it anyway, but I would venture to say that most do not. It is, in my opinion, rude for anyone in any kind of industry to use acronyms, certain words, catchphrases, and so on to anyone outside the industry.

Here is an example of a "conversation" between an agent and a client:

> *As soon as I have completed an exterior BPO I'll make an appointment to do an interior CMA. We will get an RLA signed; once you go on, the MLS agents will just use a SUPRA. Any RPAs that come in will be reviewed; last thing I want is to have to go BOM. I'll make sure the buyer is okay with their PITI and hopefully they won't have to have MI. I'll ask the lender about FREDDIE and FANNIE. I would suggest you purchase an HPP. I'm sure glad we don't have an HOA to deal with all their CCRs! Escrow will make sure a CD is taken care of before COE.*

(Betcha know this acronym; OMG!) Don't think for a minute that some presumptuous agents do not conduct themselves this way; many do.

To help a little with terminology I have put together a list of some words, acronyms, and their definitions, but only the ones that I think you have a higher likelihood of coming across. I am doing this because I want you to have as much knowledge as possible while going through the process. You certainly do not need to read them now, but do keep this book handy throughout your sale just so you have some sort of reference if you do not understand something.

Disclaimer: We do not give legal or tax advice. Please consult an attorney or tax person for anything related to any legal or tax questions you may have. The below terminology is for quick reference purposes only; we cannot guarantee their accuracy. We suggest you do your own research for further information. There are certainly many, many more real estate words and terms and acronyms out there, but here're a few that my help you through the selling process.

addendum: An addition to; a document.

appraisal: A professional determination of value. Mortgage companies usually require an appraisal of the property by a licensed, disinterested party before agreeing to loan money on the property.

back on market (BOM): When a property or listing is placed back on the market after being recently removed from the market.

balloon: A mortgage where there are payments over a period of time, but the final payment is a lump sum that is quite large, compared to the previous payments.

beneficiary: The person or bank that is owed money on a property.

Blanding Team: A team of REALTORS® who give outstanding service to their clients, highly recommended!

board of REALTORS® (local): An association of REALTORS® in a specific geographic area.

broker's price opinion (BPO): The real estate broker's opinion of the expected final net sale price, determined prior to the acquisition of the property. This is not an official appraisal.

caravan: Also known as an "office tour." A walking or driving tour by a real estate sales office of listings represented by agents in the office, usually held on a set day and time.

clear title: Ownership that is free of liens, defects, and encumbrances, beyond those which the owner agrees to accept.

comparative market analysis (CMA): A study done by real estate sales agents and brokers using active, in escrow, and sold comparable properties to estimate a listing price for a property.

condominium rules and regulations (CCR): Rules of a condominium association by which owners agree to abide.

contingency: A provision in a contract requiring certain acts to be completed before the contract is binding. A seller may put a contingency in their contract stating the sale of their home is "contingent" upon their (the sellers') purchase of a replacement property.

counteroffer: The response to an offer or a bid by the seller or buyer after the original offer or bid.

deed: The document that sellers and buyers sign when transferring title to real estate. It legally transfers the property from the seller to the buyer and is then recorded by the closing agency in county records.

deed of trust: Some states use a deed of trust to convey property being held as security for a loan. This document is then conveyed to a trustee and can be used to sell, mortgage, or subdivide the property.

delinquency: Outstanding, past-due mortgage or loan payments.

disclosures: Federal, state, county, and local requirements of disclosure that the seller provides and the buyer acknowledges.

dual agent: A state-licensed individual who represents the seller and the buyer in a single transaction.

earnest money deposit: The money given to the seller at the time the offer is made as a sign of the buyer's good faith.

easement: A legal document on a certain property giving persons other than the owner the right of way, access, and limited use or enjoyment of the land involved (e.g., power companies sometimes need a right of way for power lines).

eminent domain: The right of local or state government to purchase private property for public use. Owners receive compensation based on fair market value and sometimes additional funds for the inconvenience of moving. This is legal under the Fifth Amendment of the United States Constitution.

equity: The homeowner's part of the property value over and above the outstanding balance owed to the mortgage company.

escrow: Real estate escrow means putting something, such as a deed or money, in the custody of a neutral third party until certain conditions are met. Escrow or title companies often oversee a real estate transaction, from initial deposit to final funding, to ensure a smooth process.

FHA: Federal Housing Administration. An agency of the United States Department of Housing and Urban Development (HUD) that was established in 1934 under the National Housing Act to encourage improvement in housing standards, to provide an insurance for mortgages, and to exert a stabilizing influence on the mortgage market as a whole.

fiduciary: A relationship that implies a position of trust or confidence. Among the obligations a fiduciary owes to his principal are duties of loyalty; obedience; full disclosure; the duty to use skill, care, and diligence; and the duty to account for all finances.

fixture: Personal property that has become part of the property through permanent attachment.

flipper: A buyer who quickly sells a property for a substantial profit soon after they purchased it.

forbearance: The act of refraining from taking legal action even though payment of a promissory note in a mortgage or deed of trust is in arrears.

for sale by owner (FSBO): A property that is for sale by the owner of the property.

hard money: Relatively easy money to get with simple qualifications but at a high cost.

hazard insurance: Insurance that covers losses to real estate from damages that might affect its value.

homeowners warranty protection plan (HPP): An insurance policy covering specific future repairs, should they become necessary, for a specific time period. These are often provided by the seller or builder as a condition of sale.

homeowners' association (HOA): An association with annual dues collected from residents to ensure enforcement of any covenants or restrictions that apply to the properties covered.

HUD: The United States Department of Housing and Urban Development. This is the agency responsible for enforcing the federal Fair Housing Act. Among HUD's many programs are urban renewal, public housing, rehabilitation loans, FHA subsidy programs, and water and sewer grants. The Office of Interstate Land Sales Registration, the Federal Housing Administration (FHA), and the National Mortgage Association (GMNA) are all under HUD.

impound account: An account used to hold the funds received for payment of future bills. A lender may set up an impound account to pay taxes and insurance.

independent contractor: A real estate sales agent who conducts real estate business through a broker. This agent does not receive salary or benefits from the broker.

key box: Also referred to as a lockbox. A tool that allows secure storage of property keys on the premises for agent use.

lease purchase: A contract between a tenant and an owner by which part of the monthly rent payments may go toward down payment on the property. When predetermined sufficient funds are received by the seller, the buyer may seek a first mortgage through a typical lender or in some cases with the seller.

legal description: The written description of a piece of land giving all pertinent information such as land lot, subdivision name, block, parcel, acreage, and so on that comprises a legal and sufficient description of a particular property.

lessee: The person to whom property is rented or leased, called a tenant in most residential leases.

lessor: The person who rents or leases property to another, often referred to as a landlord, in residential leasing. One who leases property to a tenant.

lien: A monetary claim against a property that must be paid off when a property is sold in order for the new ownership to be legally recorded in county records.

lis pendens: Latin for "suit pending." A notification filed on a property stating that a legal claim has been made against the subject property.

listing agent: The real estate sales agent who is representing the sellers and their property, through a listing agreement.

listing agreement: A document that establishes the real estate agent's agreement with the sellers to represent their property in the market.

lockbox: Also referred to as a "key box." See definition for key box.

MLS: An acronym for multiple listing service. MLS is composed of hundreds of database computer systems located throughout the United States for real estate agents to showcase their available real estate listings that are for sale and for lease.

mortgage: A legal document signed by borrower(s) and promising a property to the lender in return for payment of a debt. Some states use First Trust Deeds instead of mortgages.

mortgage banker: A lender who originates mortgage loans through mortgage brokers for sale to investors.

mortgage broker: A company that buys mortgages from mortgage bankers to sell to investors such as Fannie Mae and Freddie Mac.

mortgagor: The borrower signing the note in a mortgage loan process.

multiple listing service (MLS): See definition for MLS.

National Association of REALTORS® (NAR): A national association comprising real estate professionals.

notary public: An official of integrity appointed to serve the public as an impartial witness in performing a variety of official fraud-deterrent acts related to the signing of important documents.

pending: A real estate contract that has been accepted on a property, but the transaction has not closed.

PITI: Acronym for "Principal, Interest, Taxes, and Insurance." The four parts that make up a borrower's monthly mortgage payment.

planned unit development (PUD): Mixed-use development that sets aside areas for residential use, commercial use, and public areas such as schools, parks, and so on.

principal: The amount of money a buyer borrows.

real estate owned (REO): Real estate that is owned by a bank or financial group. Usually a result of their borrowers defaulting on the loan and the subsequent foreclosure of the property from that buyer.

REALTOR®: A real estate broker or a real estate agent who holds active membership in a local board of REALTORS® that is affiliated with the National Association of REALTORS® (or NAR). The NAR has a code of ethics that all members are to adhere to. All REALTORS® are real estate brokers and real estate salespeople, but not all real estate brokers and real estate salespeople are REALTORS® (members of the National Association of REALTORS®).

refinancing: Obtaining a different loan for the benefit of perhaps a lower interest rate, converting an ARM to a fixed rate, or to take out some of the equity in the property. The borrower reapplies for a mortgage and goes through another closing transaction on the property they have previously mortgaged.

reserves: Money that mortgage companies set aside in separate non-interest-bearing accounts to pay taxes, homeowners' association dues, and insurance premiums.

right of first refusal: The right to the first opportunity to lease or purchase real property. For example, apartment tenants might retain the right of first refusal when their units are being converted to condominiums.

sign rider: An additional sign placed on a brokerage yard sign; it may include the agent's name; the words "Contract Pending" or "SOLD"; the new price; and so on.

squatter: An individual who settles on the land of another person without any legal authority to do so or without acquiring a legal title.

subordination clause: A clause in which the holder of a mortgage permits a subsequent mortgage to take priority.

Supra: An electronic lockbox (ELB) that holds keys to a property. The user must have a Supra keypad to use the lockbox.

tax lien: A lien against a property for unpaid taxes.

title insurance: An insurance company that ensures the property being sold has clear title.

trustee: The person or corporation that will carry out the wishes of another.

trustor: One who owes money to a beneficiary.

VA: United States Department of Veterans Affairs.

virtual tour: An Internet web-based video presentation of a property.

FINAL NOTE FROM THE AUTHOR AND CONTACT/LICENSE INFORMATION*

If you are located in our service area listed below and are thinking of selling your home or perhaps just have some real estate–related question, we would love to hear from you! Our assistant will put you directly in touch with us.

If you are *not* in our service area, please feel free to reach out to us anyway; our team would welcome the opportunity to help you find a like-minded agent in your area. It is our sincere desire to see your goals met, where it pertains to selling your home, with the perfect real estate agent!

You can contact our office by either phone or e-mail.
Assistant@blandingteam.com
1-888-688-4189
Visit us at Blandingteam.com

Our service areas in Southern California are as follows:
All of Los Angeles county
All of Orange county
A large part of San Bernardino and Riverside counties

We have had the privilege of serving our clients as top producers for over thirty years. I hope this book has given you some positive direction in choosing the right real estate agent to sell your home. I truly hope you are successful in that choice and that your real estate transaction is not only profitable but a positive and fruitful experience!

* If your property is currently listed with another broker, please disregard this offer. It is not our intention to solicit the offerings of other brokers.

Dan Blanding and Joy Cross
The Blanding Team
Department of Real Estate License
Numbers 00874833 and 00915798
Remax Masters Realty
DRE: 01064901